BEHIND THE BADGE

FROM POLICE CHIEF TO OPIOID ADDICT: A TRUE STORY OF RUIN AND REDEMPTION

SCOTT FLEUTER

BEHIND THE BADGE

Copyright © 2025 by Scott Fleuter

Disclaimer

The information contained in this book is provided for general informational and educational purposes only. While the author and publisher have made every effort to ensure the accuracy and completeness of the information contained herein, they assume no responsibility for errors, inaccuracies, omissions, or any outcomes that may arise from the use of this information.

This book is not intended as a substitute for professional or medical advice. Readers should consult qualified professionals for specific advice or services appropriate to their individual circumstances. Neither the author nor the publisher shall be liable for any loss or damage, directly or indirectly, caused or alleged to be caused by or in connection with the use of or reliance on any information contained in this book.

ISBN: 978-1-963705-35-5

Published in the United States of America by Harbor Lane Books, LLC.

www.harborlanebook.com

This is for you Lori.
Your love is stronger than my fears.
Your spirit, stronger than my demons.

"Behind the Badge is raw, riveting, and profoundly human. Scott Fleuter takes us from the command post to the abyss and back again with unflinching honesty and unexpected grace. His story shatters stigma and reminds us that even in the darkest fall, there's a way back to light."

— *Lara Love Hardin, New York Times bestselling author of The Many Lives of Mama Love*

"Inviting, honest, and utterly compelling. Scott Fleuter is a masterful storyteller, and this book belongs on every shelf."

— *C.J. Redwine, New York Times bestselling author of The Shadow Queen*

"Scott's book is a raw and inspiring testament to the grueling journey of overcoming opioid addiction while navigating the intense pressures of working in law-enforcement. The unflinching honesty with which he portrays his struggles—balancing the weight of his professional responsibilities with the relentless grip of addiction—lends a gritty realism that resonates deeply. His vivid storytelling captures the despair, resilience, and ultimate triumph of his path to sobriety, making it a powerful read for anyone seeking hope or understanding of addiction's complexities. The transformation to a happy, productive life shines through as a beacon of possibility, inspiring readers with its authenticity and hard-earned optimism."

— *Bill Reynolds, PA-C*

Director of Military and First Responder Trauma Recovery Program - Sierra Tucson

"The devastation Scott experienced through our society's over-prescribing of drugs, combined with the traumas he experienced during his career, captured my heart.

Behind the Badge provides law enforcement professionals, their families, loved ones, and anyone dealing with drug addiction and depression, valuable tools to help them recover and live again."

— Laura Zeliff, Ret. Deputy Chief, Grants Pass Department of Public Safety

Ret. Police Academy Coordinator, Rogue Community College

INTRODUCTION

I was cloistered in my apartment bathroom, staring into a half-empty bottle of oxycodone. The seductive white capsules were supposed to last for a month. I'd taken half in less than one week. I stuck the bottle of meds into a plastic bag, wrapped the bag in an entire roll of tape, and stuffed the package into the back corner of my bedroom closet shelf. The pills were gone in two days.

———

I'm an opioid addict. This is a story about my slow spiral into addiction and the cruel road to recovery. It's about being in constant pain and suffering from severe mental illness. And, it's about the rollercoaster ride out of the depths of addiction.

No one grows up wanting to be a junkie, but some of us grow up unconsciously paving the way to addiction. I didn't have an abusive upbringing. All my basic needs for shelter, food, clothes, and security were met by a nurturing mother and a decent, yet emotionally unavailable, father. I never went hungry a day in my life. And when it comes to privilege, I did the DNA spit test: I'm a genetic mutt of German, Scandinavian, and British descent. That's about as white as one can get. Even so, I still managed to slip into the iron grip of addiction. Opioids do not discriminate.

For many years, I was able to function at a reasonably high level, pun intended. I pursued a demanding career in law enforcement that led to a position as Chief of Police in Ashland, Oregon, a progressive college town in the mountains of the Northwest. I have a Master's Degree, taught at the local university, and traveled around the nation assessing other law enforcement agencies for their accreditation status.

I still got hooked on opioids and lost my career, health, and every shred of my self-worth. The shame and self-loathing alone were unbearable. I was in a hole so deep that I couldn't see even a pinprick of light at the top.

It took a long time, but I was able to climb out of that hole and start down the road to recovery. And, I didn't do it alone. In my experience, no one can recover from something as powerful as opioid addiction without the love and support of family and friends, as well as help from professionals in the field of substance use disorders. All I had to do was ask.

My mission with *Behind the Badge* is to ignite a spark of hope for readers who are addicts or recovering addicts; to foster the courage it takes to make big changes in life, even if the odds seem insurmountable; and to rekindle faith in a world where despair has become the rule. If I can prevent one person from becoming hooked on opioids, or if I can guide them through the horror show of recovery, then I will have met my goal.

This book is also for families and close friends of addicts. It's frustrating and distressing to love an addict. No one wants to be stuck with the physical and emotional wreckage we leave in our wake.

Finally, this book is for anyone working in the field of trauma, mental health, or addiction. In my mind, the three cannot be separated. I have never met an addict who didn't have some underlying trauma that led to misusing substances as a coping mechanism, or who didn't have some form of anxiety, depression, or post-traumatic stress disorder. Although some of my best counselors were recovering addicts, that doesn't mean that a non-addict counselor can't be equally effective. My intent is to provide some additional insight from the client's perspective for those folks brave enough to work in the fields of trauma and mental health.

My hope is to shed some light on the taboos, misconceptions, and stigmas of addiction in general, and the opioid crisis in particular. I'm focusing on opioids because it's what I know best. As a retired police officer and an opioid addict, I've lived on both sides of the drug epidemic fence. It is clear to me that arresting and incarcerating people with addiction and/or mental health problems is counterproductive and inhumane.

I've gained more knowledge than I ever wanted on all sorts of destructive behavior. This includes folks with eating disorders, alcoholism, sex addicts, cutters, gamblers, hoarders, obsessive shoppers, and adrenaline junkies. And, if I were to make a prediction, obsessive use of social media will soon be on the official list. Addiction is addiction.

Each chapter in this book includes a story from my journey, along with therapy sessions led by a counselor of my creation (she is a conglomeration of all the good therapists I've encountered over the years). The final part of each chapter provides a practical application section with tips, techniques, and advice for managing addiction.

Part One of *Behind the Badge* consists of stories, mostly from my childhood, that illustrate how our brains and bodies can become insidiously wired for addiction. It includes events and sessions that detail how my personal values were engraved upon my brain, much like a river gradually carving a canyon through the earth.

Part Two includes life stories and events that led to my slow spiral into addiction, chronic pain, and severe depression. It covers the rise and fall of a successful law enforcement career, along with the years after I lost my job and plunged so deeply into despair that suicide seemed the only way out.

Part Three is supported by stories and sessions relating to the rollercoaster ride of the recovery process. It shines a light on how connections with other people, as well as being in nature, play a critical role in healing from trauma and addiction.

PART ONE

Hard-Wired for Addiction

CHAPTER
ONE
FIGHT VS. FLIGHT

The kid picked up a wooden 2"x4" and took a swing at my head. Like spikes on a medieval mace, three huge nails protruded from the end of the board. I leapt back as the crude weapon barely missed my nose. This was supposed to be a fistfight. At least, that's what my six-year-old brain thought.

A solid ring of grade-school boys surrounded me and my attacker. They shouted like a crowd of spectators at a Roman coliseum, eager for first blood. I took a quick glance to the side and saw a couple of the bigger kids holding back my brother, Mark, who was attempting to rush to my aid. Mark was three years my senior, but he was overmatched by sheer numbers.

I was on my own.

The battle took place in a large field choked with ragged weeds and assorted junk discarded by people unwilling to pay the dump fees. It was less than a football field's length from the unfenced backyards of the modest middle-class suburb that was home to everyone in attendance. All it would take was just one parent to glance out of their window, see the seething ring of boys, and know that something was amiss.

But that didn't happen.

I backpedaled a couple of yards, and the kid rushed forward, holding the spiked weapon over his head like a sword. The wild look in his eyes scared me almost as much as the board whistling straight down toward my skull. I jumped to my right, lost my footing, and sprawled onto the ground. The board smacked the dirt, but left me unscathed.

I'd landed on top of a long, green piece of bamboo. I scooped up the pole and sprang to my feet while the kid struggled to free his makeshift weapon from the hard-packed earth where the nails had impaled it.

During that split second, my mind tried to make sense of the situation. I was the youngest member of what the boys in my neighborhood called the Pine Street Army, named after the street where we lived. My opponent was the youngest member of the Willow Street Army, which was made up of kids from a street a couple of blocks away. Our two armies had been feuding all summer, and we were at a stalemate. Unbeknownst to me, the older kids had decided to let the two of us fight it out. The winner's army could then claim victory for the season, before school started up next week.

Pine's base of operations was a small hill in a field behind our houses. It was originally a huge pile of dirt left from some building project long since abandoned. Now, it was covered by tall, green weeds and riddled with a series of foxholes. Right across the street, the Willow gang commanded a massive pit—most likely the original source of our own dirt pile—warded by a corrugated metal wall scavenged from the surrounding field.

The Pine Street vs. Willow Street war had been raging for months. It had started out innocently enough, at least for young boys who tended to do stupid things. We'd discovered that pulling up bunches of the long green grass that covered our hill resulted in a formidable weapon with an impressive clump of dark-brown dirt attached to the end. We'd spin them overhead and send the projectiles flying over the street to either impact Willow's metal wall with a satisfying bang or, better yet, score a hit on one of our enemies. Of course, they did the same thing, and sometimes the air was full of little brown comets with trails of green flame.

But much like nations at war, our violence had escalated from swinging fists and throwing dirt clods to a battle for survival.

I watched as my opponent freed his weapon and rushed straight at me. I swung the bamboo pole like a skinny baseball bat and struck the 2"x4". Fueled by adrenaline, my blow sent the board flying from his grip.

Driven by a rage so deep that it blocked out any notion of humanity, I threw down the pole and leaped at my adversary. I drove him to the ground, straddled his chest, and pummeled his face with my fists. Red droplets rained down, soaking into the grass. A few of the older kids from each side rushed in and finally pulled me off.

So, I guess we won.

Therapy Session

I hated telling that story. And, I hated sitting in a psychologist's office being analyzed by some shrink who'd never suffered through the horrors of opioid addiction.

Ursula Schmidt, Ph.D., sat back and narrowed her jade-green eyes. "Pretty heavy experience for a six-year-old," she said.

"It was," I replied. "I didn't even really remember it until a few years ago." My hands began to sweat, and I wiped them on my jeans. I had a powerful urge to bolt out the door.

"And that was your first memory of violence?" Dr. Schmidt asked. She was a trim, handsome woman with a slight German accent. No wedding ring, but I could see a faint tan line on that finger.

"First one that came to mind. My parents never beat me or anything, if that's what you mean." I felt sweat dampening my armpits and beading up on my forehead.

We faced each other, ensconced in overstuffed chairs. No obligatory couch, and no barrier filling the two-foot gap between us. Ursula handed me a box of tissues.

"No, I didn't mean that at all," she said. "It just seems that if you had an ongoing conflict with those Willow Street kids, there would be other incidents of violence."

"Tons," I agreed. "I remember one time when a kid punched me in the face, and my nose started pouring blood. I just kept on swinging anyway, and I guess it must have freaked him out because he ran away."

I wiped my forehead with the tissue and crumpled it tightly in my fist. What if she thought I was a violent psychopath? My heart began to thump against my ribs.

Using one of the orienting skills I'd learned in rehab, I took a few deep breaths and concentrated on scanning her office. The exposed brick walls were adorned with artwork of red-rock canyons, desert sunsets, and other splendors that dominated the southwest.

"How old were you when you got the bloody nose?" she asked, scribbling a few more notes on her pad.

"It was before that board-with-the-nails thing," I replied. "Probably when I was in kindergarten." My eyes were drawn to a bouquet of bright yellow daffodils sprouting from a tall crystal vase. The flowers were set on an old wooden desk that'd likely been there since the place was built.

Ursula set the pad down on a small table next to

her chair and ran one hand through her short blond hair. She was dressed in a black skirt and a royal blue sleeveless blouse.

"Where were your mom and dad when all of these things were happening?" she asked. "Were you reprimanded by the parents of the kid who attacked you with the board?"

"Nope, not at all. My parents never heard about either, as far as I know. I had great parents. Well, my dad was emotionally unavailable for the most part. He was one of those Normandy WWII veterans who didn't say much. But Mom and Dad worked full-time. My brother and I pretty much ran wild."

I realized that I still had a death grip on the tissue wadded up in my fist. I relaxed my grip and stuffed the damp Kleenex into my pants pocket. I sat back and tried to relax, letting my body sink into the overstuffed chair.

"My dad got a new job later that year, in San Francisco, so we moved to California."

"I'd like to talk about that during our next session, and more of your family history," Ursula said. "Since this is our first session, do you have any questions or concerns so far that you'd like to talk about?" she asked.

I took a slow, deep breath and let it out. "I guess even after all these years of therapy and treatment, I still don't know why this all happened to me. It's not like I was abused as a child or had parents who were addicts."

I could feel my face getting hot. I took a few more

steady breaths and dropped my shoulders. "I know it sounds like whining, but I just can't seem to get over the 'why me' thing."

Ursula ignored my self-deprecation.

"Why *not* you?" she asked. "As far as the 'how,' it could be a combination of many things. Genetics, your environment, life experiences, the decisions you make—they all come into play."

"But I don't even really know what came first," I said. "It's like the chicken or the egg dilemma. Did the drugs cause my depression, or was I already depressed?"

"We're going to sort all that out. But the first thing you can work on is dropping the 'why,' or it could drive you bonkers."

"Too late," I said, not missing a beat.

Ursula laughed. It was a pleasant laugh. I was relieved she had a sense of humor. My new therapist seemed to be a strange fit for a small town tucked into the mountains of New Mexico, where PhDs numbered in the single digits and faded blue jeans and Stetsons dominated the local fashion scene.

I noticed that my heart rate had slowed back down to normal. The orienting techniques were working. Not long ago, I couldn't even get in the door of a doctor's office without it triggering a major anxiety attack.

I'd come a long way.

"Childhood is a great place to start on the 'how' question," she said. "In your case, one of your core beliefs was that you weren't safe and that it was up to you to fight and defend yourself. You assumed that no one was going to help and that you were completely on your own."

Pretty astute for a first session, I thought.

"That was definitely my experience, and not just as a kid. When I feel threatened, I tend to go straight to fight mode."

"That's good insight." Ursula nodded. "I would think that you also felt a sense of abandonment when no one came to your rescue. That's another core belief we can discuss later."

Once again, she'd hit the mark. Maybe I *did* need this.

"Reprogramming your brain takes a lot of time and work," she said. "And, in your case, you've become what some might call an adrenaline junkie. You've been exposed to not only violence but the excitement and rush that goes along with it."

"Do you think that's why I became a cop?"

"I do," she confirmed. "You feel most alive when you place yourself in dangerous situations. You thrive on chaos and reckless behavior. Your brain is wired for addiction and depression."

Speaking of brains, mine was exhausted. She seemed to pick up on it.

"And, I think that's plenty to cover for our first session."

Survival Tips

Until it happened to me, I never would've believed someone could spin into a panic attack without warning. As a police officer, it seemed perfectly natural to face an armed criminal. Now, after being addicted to opioids, my body can't tell the difference between a real and an imagined threat. I can spiral into fight or flight mode because of something as small as waiting in a doctor's office or getting stuck in traffic.

However, before I get into tips, techniques, and advice on dealing with stress and anxiety, it's important to learn how to **belly breathe** (diaphragmatic breathing). The diaphragm muscle is the one between the stomach and the lungs. It is attached to the bottom of the lungs and acts like a bellows to draw air into the lungs.

Belly breathing can be done lying down, sitting, or standing. It can even be done while walking, but I would wait to try that until you have a firm grasp on the technique.

As you draw in your breath, resist the urge to expand your upper chest. Instead, draw your diaphragm muscle downward and outward. It may feel a bit like your stomach is filling with air. Release the air from your lungs by completely relaxing your diaphragm muscle.

Repeat.

Belly breathing can be used for a number of mindfulness techniques, such as scanning, yoga, qigong, and meditation. This is how babies breathe. We've just forgotten how.

Scanning: One of the stress reduction techniques I learned in rehab was to ground myself by scanning my surroundings. It was helpful during the emotional roller coaster ride of opioid withdrawal.

Take a few slow, deep belly breaths. Drop your shoulders. It seems anytime I need this technique, I'm indoors and sitting down. Wherever you are, get comfortable and continue the belly breathing.

Look around and notice things like artwork on the wall, a light switch, a chair, a vase of flowers, and so on. It's best to slowly turn your head versus just moving your eyes. No need to linger—just move on to the next visual distraction. Remember to drop your shoulders. Keep going until your heart rate settles down.

Scanning can be done alone or in a group setting. It can even be done in line at the grocery store when you're stuck behind that customer with all the coupons. My attacks seem to always happen indoors, so it's a good incentive to get out in nature.

Modified 4-Count Breathing: Another technique I use for reducing anxiety is four-count breathing. Breathe in through your nose for four seconds. Breathe out through your mouth for four seconds. Expel any excess air out of your lungs. Hold your breath for four seconds. It's important to hold your breath at the end of the exhale, not between the inhale and exhale. This may feel odd at first, but I find it much more relaxing.

Ice Cubes: This technique will draw a bit more attention than scanning the room, but a little social embarrassment is much better than spending hours suffering while your heart feels like it's about to explode. The goal is to be aware of the present (my freezing hand) instead of focusing on the impending panic attack.

Grab a handful of ice cubes and head outside. Find a hard surface like cement or asphalt.

Squeeze the cubes until the ache is intense and your knuckles are turning white. Throw the cubes on the ground as hard as you can.

Sounds weird, but it works.

The above techniques aren't just for panic attacks. They can also be used as distraction techniques for surfing the urge (cravings) for drugs or reckless behavior. Panic attacks are terrifying and, for me, can cause complete paralysis. During my first one, I was sure it was a heart attack. My first two major panic attacks took place in a rehab facility and a psych ward, and both times the staff called for the EKG crash-cart to make sure it wasn't a heart attack. So, if you've never experienced one, you'll need to have trained medical personnel rule out a heart attack or other medical emergency.

Unfortunately, one of the main challenges that accompanies addiction is that the mental health issues, such as depression and anxiety, may never go away. That's why, when the level of stress is high enough to trigger an attack, it's so important to practice techniques—even simple ones—like the ones mentioned in this chapter.

A panic attack can often be avoided if it's caught early enough. But if your symptoms become overwhelming, it may be too late for the above techniques, in which case, your best bet is to just lie down and belly breathe.

CHAPTER
TWO
BRAIN GROOVING

Therapy Session

"Last session, we talked about some traumatic events that may have started you down the road to addiction and depression," Dr. Schmidt recapped. "I think it's clear that some of your experiences as a little boy gave you a taste for adrenaline."

"Addicted to the rush," I said as I looked around her sunlit office. We sat in the same comfortable chairs. The daffodils had been replaced by white daisies with bright yellow centers.

"Exactly," she agreed. "Those events shaped your values and beliefs. Especially the belief that you were on your own and that no one was going to help you."

I felt my body tense. My first session with Dr. Schmidt had gone okay, but the topic of being abandoned was a drama that saturated my entire life.

I concentrated on the late morning sunlight

streaming through the window. It highlighted Ursula's short blond hair. There were strands of silver in the mix. Today, she wore a lavender half-sleeve top and pants the color of butter.

She set her writing pad on the table, leaned forward, and looked me in the eye.

"In your young mind, you were betrayed," she explained. "And that seems to be a recurring theme for you."

I suddenly felt like a coiled spring. The urge to run out the door was even stronger than it had been during my first visit. I sank lower into the chair and crossed my arms over my chest.

"What's going on in your mind right now, Scott?"

"Betrayal," I answered. "That word always sets me off, I guess."

"Why do you think that is?"

"Because I wasn't just betrayed as a kid. I was betrayed during my career. I was betrayed by all the brilliant doctors who hooked me on opioids. I was betrayed by my own body and mind."

Once again, I felt my heart start to thump against my rib cage—a sure sign of an impending panic attack. I tried to unwind, to orient, but to no avail.

Ursula relaxed back into her chair. We sat in silence for a moment.

"I noticed in your medical history that you received Somatic Experiencing Therapy for releasing stored trauma," she said. "What did you think of it?"

I kept my arms firmly locked around my chest in a

vain effort to calm my heart. "It works," I managed to choke out.

"When we first talked on the phone," Ursula continued, "I remember I told you I'm certified in Somatic Experiencing Therapy."

"I remember."

"Would you like to do a session right now, Scott?"

It felt like a truckload of bricks was pressing on my chest. I'd become comfortable with the Somatic Experiencing therapist I'd had back during rehab. But I'd just met Dr. Schmidt. Could I trust her?

"It's completely your choice," she added. "We could try it another time. But, I think it would be helpful for you right now."

I didn't have a choice. I couldn't face a meltdown. "Let's do it."

Ursula got up and partially closed the blinds on the large window. "Are you okay with some aromatherapy?" she asked.

I uncrossed my arms. "Sure."

She walked over to a large wooden cabinet, opened it, and selected a small vial of essential oil from an impressive collection. "I'm not sure what you used in the past, but this feels right," she said as she came back and sat next to me. She opened the vial and held it near my nose. "What do you think?"

I took a long inhale and dropped my shoulders. Cedar. Perfect. My heartbeat seemed to slow down immediately.

"This is exactly what my therapist used in rehab.

She even gave me a small cloth soaked in cedar oil to carry around with me. How did you know?"

"I didn't." Ursula put some dabs of the fragrant oil on the inside of both of my wrists. "I'll give you some to take home. Rub your wrists together a little."

She got up, went back to the cabinet, and removed a blanket.

"This is a weighted blanket. Have you ever used one?"

"I have."

Once again, Dr. Schmidt made the right call. I'd always used a weighted blanket in the past. It made me feel more secure. She draped the soft blanket over my body and sat back in her chair.

"Try relaxing your shoulders a little more," she counseled. "You can keep your hands under the blanket or on top, but just let them relax in your lap."

I followed her directions and closed my eyes. The spicy aroma of cedar filled the air. I felt the muscles in my arms and chest begin to uncoil. It was amazing how a simple smell could be so powerful.

"Now, concentrate on your breath," Ursula said. "I'm sure you've learned how to belly breathe. Do that, and let it fill up your entire body."

I already had a lot of time in the Somatic Experiencing chair, and it didn't take long for my heartbeat to level out. It was still thumping away like a bass drum, but the rhythm was slowing.

"Because you've done this before," she said, "you may already have a safe place to go to. Or, you can create a new one. Take your time and bring that image to mind. When you're ready, describe the place to me."

I took a deep breath. "I'm sitting on a grassy bank next to a small, sun-dappled creek. The creek wanders through a grove of evergreens."

"Are you alone?" she asked.

"My wife is there. She's sitting to my left, just inside my peripheral vision. It's warm, but there's a cooling breeze that carries the voice of the creek to my ears."

Neither of us spoke for a moment.

"Stay there and keep focusing on your breathing," Ursula directed.

A couple of minutes passed, and I felt the crushing weight lift from my chest.

"How do you feel, Scott?"

Then came the tears. They streamed down my face like my imaginary creek. Sobs wracked my chest. Cathartic, cleansing tears washed away layer after layer of anxiety and stress. Ursula slid the trusty Kleenex box my way. Then, she just sat back and let me be. I concentrated on slowing down my breathing and reached for a generous handful of tissues.

"Would you like to stop for today?" she asked. "We still have plenty of time, but it's your call."

I mopped my face and disposed of the sodden Kleenex in the wire-mesh trash can next to her wooden desk.

"No," I replied. "A couple of years ago, that attack would've taken me out for three days." I pulled the weighted blanket off my chest but left it covering my legs. The motion sent a pleasant waft of cedar my way.

"But not now?"

"No. Not now," I said. "I think it's okay to keep going. I feel a lot better."

"You look a lot better." Ursula picked up her yellow writing pad. "I'm glad you want to go on. And, the fact that you recovered so quickly is huge progress."

I removed the blanket from my legs, folded it up, and set it on the small table next to my chair. "Where to now?" I asked.

Ursula's green eyes sparkled. "I want to explore your childhood a little more. Maybe talk about other violent traumas that came into your life. Last session, you said your family moved to California when you were in elementary school. Did you continue to get in fights after the move?"

"Oh, yeah," I replied. "In fact, probably even more. I learned early that if you hit fast and hard, the fight is over before it begins."

"Tell me about an incident that stands out in your mind."

———

My best friend, Jack, fit an arrow to his bow.

"What are you doing?" I asked. "You can't shoot at those guys with that."

He lowered his bow. "You're right. I'd probably lose my arrow."

That wasn't what I meant. I was thinking along the lines of not killing one of the six kids rushing up the hill. Even though we were vastly outnumbered, I thought we'd have a hard time explaining why an eight-year-old boy had an arrow stuck in his eye. Granted, it was one of those practice arrows with a pointed metal cap on the tip, not one of the wicked razor-edged ones used for slaying deer, but we didn't have time for a discussion on tactics or morals. Although we held the high ground on top of a big hill, our adversaries were more than halfway up the slope and well-armed with sticks and slingshots.

This particular confrontation was the result of a feud we'd had with a group of kids who all lived in a cul-de-sac a couple of blocks from Jack's house. It started when my best friend and I formed what we called the Cougar Club.

There were only two members.

We were in third grade, and I'd recently moved from Utah to a town on the fringes of the Bay Area. We were into cougars—the animal, not older ladies— for no other reason than the fact that we'd seen Walt Disney's movie *Cougar Country*, which followed the life of a couple of cougar cubs into adulthood.

Thus, the Cougar Club.

"Let's just stick to slingshots," I said, pulling mine out of the back pocket of my Levi's and picking up a marble-sized rock.

Jack did the same, and we launched a few volleys at the kids as they labored up the hill. We scored a few hits, including one kid who fell to his knees when struck in the cheek, but our attackers were still too far away for the little rocks to do more than just slow them down.

"This isn't working too well," Jack observed. "What should we do?"

"We still have our secret weapon," I replied. "After all the work it took to set it up, we might as well use it."

It was a bold move. We didn't hate these kids. It was more a matter of honor. Shortly after the inception of the Cougar Club, we'd made a flag out of an old sheet sporting a passable drawing of a cougar head. The flag flew on a long pole above our clubhouse—a dilapidated shack in Jack's side yard. A couple of weeks ago, the gang of boys currently running up the hill had seen the flag and felt it was appropriate to lob large rocks over the fence. Some of those rocks landed on the metal roof of our clubhouse. This happened more than once.

On the last occasion, we were in the shack and spied them running away. One thing led to another, and after a few verbal engagements in the schoolyard, it was decided that we'd meet on top of Sliding Hill to fight it out at noon that Saturday. Jack and I got there a little early.

"Let's do it," Jack said.

The secret weapon was a large log with dozens of

bowling ball-sized rocks heaped up behind it. The log ran parallel to the edge of the flat top of the hill and was held in place by a couple of stakes we'd driven into the ground.

By now, the group of boys was only about fifty yards away. We pulled out the stakes and let loose a small landslide. The log swung to one side, but the tumbling rocks picked up momentum and were right on target.

Two of the kids got their legs knocked out from under them and began to roll down the hill. The other four took a few hits as well. They'd had enough and finally fled down the hill almost as fast as the pursuing rocks.

We never had any problems with those guys after that.

Therapy Session cont.

"Let me guess," Ursula said. "No parents found out about that either."

"If they did, I never heard about it." I shrugged. "Just like in Utah, both of my parents worked full-time."

She nodded. "At the time of the fight on the hill, did you believe Jack would've really shot someone with an arrow? It seems a little extreme."

I looked around her brick-walled office as I

thought about it. There were no photographs of her family. I didn't even know if she had one.

"You know, to this day, I'm not sure if Jack would've fired that arrow," I said. "But it doesn't take long for young boys to switch into *Lord of the Flies* mode."

"An apt analogy," she replied. "How did you meet Jack?"

"During a fight. I'd just started third grade and, like boys everywhere, I had to prove myself, I guess. He and another kid started taunting me on the playground. I was a little incredulous since I was bigger and stronger than both of them. I punched out the other kid and grabbed Jack by the front of his shirt. I remember he said, 'Hey, let go. You're stretching the material.' It cracked me up, so I let him go. We became fast friends after that."

"I guess that's one way to make friends. I never thought I'd say this, but I think I'm glad I had a daughter," Ursula commented, showing the first glimpse into her personal life. Sharing that little bit of her life made her more human in my eyes.

My whole body relaxed another notch.

"How were your grades in elementary school?" she asked.

"I squeaked by with mostly D's in grade school, but never got held back. I think that was because some of my teachers didn't want me in their classroom a second time."

She laughed at that.

"I know you have a master's degree, and that you

were a police chief, and taught at the college level. Obviously, you're intelligent. Why do you think you were a poor student back then?'"

"That's a good question," I replied. "Even to get the D's, I remember stealing my fifth-grade teacher's edition of our math book—you know, the one with all the answers after the questions. I was way behind on my work and spent a few recesses hidden away somewhere to catch up. But, I did return the copy to my teacher's desk."

As if that redeemed what I had done, I thought.

"I guess I really don't know why I got low grades. I was so focused on sports and anything physical. I was always one of the fastest and strongest kids in grade school."

"You were a successful athlete," Ursula said. "But lots of kids who are good at sports do fine with academics. Why else do you think you got poor grades?"

I racked my brain and closed my eyes for a moment, trying to dig deep.

"I guess I had a problem with authority. I always dug my heels in whenever a teacher tried to make me do something."

Ursula jotted down some notes on her pad.

"A police chief with authority problems?" she asked with a smile.

"I know it sounds weird. I've been through a lot of counseling and treatment over the years, and I'm beginning to think that one of the reasons I became a cop, besides the rush, was that I thought I might as well *be* the authority. I think that was also what drove me to become a police chief. I don't like other people telling me what to do."

"So, you'd rather be the one in ultimate control?"

"Exactly," I said, imagining that she wrote "control freak" on her pad.

"Do you think you're a perfectionist?" she asked.

"Like a neat freak? Nah, no way. I think my wife would say I'm pretty good at making messes. Especially in the kitchen."

Ursula smiled, causing subtle laugh lines at the corners of her eyes. The sign of a perpetual smiler.

"No," she said. "More like thinking if it's going to be done right, you'd better do it yourself. Or even having to be the best at everything you do, poor grades aside."

I smiled back. "It wasn't that many years ago that I actually believed I was the best at everything I did."

"Do you feel that way now?" she asked.

"I'm much more humble these days."

Survival Tips

Addictions are based, in part, on some form of past trauma constantly invading our present lives. There are proven therapies to reduce that trauma and allow healing to move forward. They work for me, and they can work for you.

When I first started seeking help for my pain and

addiction, re-grooving the brain was a hard concept to grasp. I understood the original grooving of my brain, but getting the old habits and reactions to leave that groove seemed far-fetched.

An image that stands out in my mind is of water slowly carving its way into the earth. Even the Grand Canyon started as a shallow river. Our brains are like that. And my canyons of addiction and trauma seemed bottomless.

Somatic Experiencing: Somatic Experiencing therapy (SE) should only be done with a certified practitioner. It would also help to work with a therapist or primary care physician before venturing into any modalities that deal with stored trauma.

Somatic Experiencing is partly based on the realization that other animals shake off stress and are able to return to their normal state. We humans tend to let shame and judgment override the body's natural response to dispel the adrenaline rush. The result of all this stored trauma can often manifest itself in anxiety attacks, hypervigilance, and aggression. After several SE sessions, I was able to recognize the stress and tension in parts of my body, so I could work on discharging that tension on my own.

During my first Somatic Experiencing therapy session, my counselor sat me in a big, padded gravity recliner, turned down the lights, and put on some soothing music. Then she covered me in a weighted blanket and dabbed some essential oils on my wrists.

Most importantly, she helped me visualize what she called my **"happy place"** to use during meditation or any other mindfulness practice. It doesn't even have to be real. My happy place is a sunny meadow studded by wildflowers next to a creek, surrounded by trees. Not only can I see the meadow, creek, and trees in my mind's eye, but I can also feel the breeze and sunshine on my skin, smell the flowers, and hear the water.

You can pull from favorite memories, or just get into a relaxed state and start to visualize a place where you wouldn't mind hanging out each day to recharge your batteries. Although it could be a subway train in New York City, if that's what's comfortable and familiar for you, I've found that, for me, nature is best. I'm a mountain, lake, and creek person (with some hot springs thrown in). But some people are drawn to a warm, palm-fringed, tropical beach, or the red-rock canyons of the Southwest, where the night skies are so pristine that you can read by starlight. Whatever you select, it should be a place where you feel at peace.

Although I can't do an SE session at home by myself, there were a few things I learned through my SE experiences that can be handy tools for managing and releasing stress.

Aromatherapy: One of my fondest childhood memories is camping in the Sierra Nevada mountains. I remember sticking my nose against the sunbaked bark of a towering ponderosa pine tree and inhaling the spicy-sweet aroma. Smells can evoke powerful memories and emotions. The scent of pine and cedar reminds me of happy days camping with my family and friends.

Essential oils are readily available at pharmacies, grocery stores, and online. Even Costco has them. Find one (or several) that make you feel good. Lavender is classic for relaxation. Citrus invigorates. Bergamot is good for anxiety. You can use an infuser, dab some on your wrists, or even put a few drops on a cotton ball to sniff as needed.

Weighted Blankets: Most of us have seen someone sitting in a group situation with a couch pillow firmly clasped to their lap. That was certainly the case during my process groups in rehab. That works, but a weighted blanket may be a better alternative. Weighted blankets help calm the nervous system, making you feel safe and secure, kind of like swaddling a baby. They can also be good for sleep because, for some, they can help the body relax.

Weighted blankets are available online and at stores such as Target, Barnes & Noble, and Big Five. Heavy pillows and quilts work in a pinch.

The above therapy and techniques can help open new neural pathways that may start as a trickle, but gradually create their own canyons. The old scars will not go away, but they become relegated to where they belong: a memory like any other memory, instead of a current traumatic event that plays over and over in your mind. Whatever technique or therapy you use to shed some of that stored trauma, expect to do a lot of cathartic crying. Embrace it. Let it out. After all, every trickle leads to a river. And every river can carve a new canyon.

CHAPTER
THREE
BRAIN MEETS DRUGS

Therapy Session

Dr. Schmidt was dressed down this time, in jeans and an olive-green t-shirt. "Did you get into physical confrontations in middle school and high school?" she asked.

We were in our usual comfortable chairs. I was starting to feel less fidgety in her office.

"I got into a bunch of fistfights in middle school, some more brutal than others," I answered. "I don't remember any serious fights in high school."

"Did you still get poor grades?"

I clasped my hands together on my lap, but kept the grip loose. Having been through a successful Somatic Experiencing session with Ursula, I was beginning to trust her.

"I remember they put me in the slow math group in middle school," I answered. "But, more C's, and even a couple of B's, started showing up on my report cards. And, once I reached high school, it was mostly A's and a few B's."

Ursula jotted a few notes down. "How about sports? I noticed in your background packet that you started getting some injuries at about age twelve or thirteen."

I was impressed that she took the time to read that packet. In my experience with counselors and doctors, it was a huge waste of time to fill that stuff out because they usually never even glanced at it.

"That's true," I said. "I played catcher all through my Little League years. I was good and became one of the starting players the year I began middle school. But all those seasons of hunkering down behind home plate finally took their toll." I leaned forward, reached down, and rubbed the back of my right calf.

"How so?"

"It was my Achilles tendons," I replied, wincing at the memory. "They were totally shot. I couldn't even crouch down without extreme pain. That was the end of baseball for me." I looked up at the ceiling, realizing for the first time that it must be about twelve feet high. I suddenly felt very small.

"Did that make you stop playing sports?"

"No, I was too stupid for that," I said as my eyes dwelled on the old ceiling. It looked to be made of metal tiles like they used 150 years ago, but it had been painted over so many times that the embossed design was blurred and indistinct. "I blew out my knee when I was a junior playing on the tennis team.

It wasn't long before more injuries followed. My athletic days were pretty much done after that."

"Loss," Ursula commented.

I pulled my eyes from the ceiling, sat up, and looked at her. "Huh?" I frowned, puzzled.

"That's a lot of loss," she explained. "And a lot of pain. When was the first time you took any painkillers that contained opioids or synthetic opioids?"

The big question.

My jaw tightened, and some old anger at the doctors gleefully shoving opioids my way boiled to the surface.

"That would have been after my knee surgery when I was sixteen," I said. My hands were still clasped in my lap, but now the knuckles were turning white. "I'd torn the cartilage in my left knee. It was back in the day when there was no such thing as arthroscopic surgery. The scar is huge. I'll never forget how good the Demerol felt flowing through my body."

"Why don't you relax your grip, Scott?" Ursula coached, noticing my tension. "Maybe shake your hands out a bit."

I followed her advice and added a couple of deep breaths.

"It was amazing how quickly the pain meds took me from excruciating pain to such an intense euphoria," I continued.

"I think we'll need at least a whole session or more to cover all your injuries and surgeries. Especially how they tied into using painkillers," Ursula said. "But, tell me about the first time you drank alcohol or used any other drugs. And, I don't mean a sip of your dad's beer."

———

It was a shocking sight, especially for a sixth grader, but right there in front of me, a fellow classmate named Mitch was on his knees, giving my friend, Ron, a blow job.

We were at a small lake way out in the boonies. There were five of us, sixth-grade boys from the same school. Mitch had stolen a bunch of beer from the local supermarket. The plan was to sneak to the isolated lake and get drunk.

It was my first time drinking, and I'd reached the point where lying in the grass with my eyes closed seemed to be a good idea, but that just made the spinning worse. Unfortunately, I opened my eyes at the wrong time and got an eyeful of the two boys. Ron suddenly yanked away and ran off. Mitch fell backward and passed out.

Earlier that afternoon, the outing to the lake sounded like a good idea. Now, things were clearly out of control. I looked around to see what the remaining two guys were up to. One was in the process of throwing the beer stealer's portable radio into the lake. The other was staggering so badly that he hit a tree and fell to the ground.

It had started with our little group sitting on the grassy bank by the lake, enjoying a sunny autumn afternoon and taking turns chugging stolen malt liquor from 40-ounce bottles. It didn't take long for the alcohol to hit our young brains. It was a blast, and we spent most of the time laughing and listening to Mitch's radio.

The one that ended up underwater.

One of the kids produced a joint from his pocket, and we added a little marijuana to the mix. Another first for me. Mitch had the bright idea to run to his house half a mile away and pilfer a full bottle of bourbon from his dad's liquor cabinet. When he got back, we drank almost the whole bottle between us before it also ended up in the middle of the lake.

I was too intoxicated to even stand up, and that's how I found myself lying in the grass watching the world spin around behind my eyelids, which, in my mind, was a lot better than watching what happened when I opened my eyes.

Let's just say it was a sobering experience.

I had the sudden urge to go home and managed to get to my feet. The sun was setting, and I knew my parents were home from work by now and were probably wondering where I was. Ron had the same idea. Mitch and the kid who ran into the tree were still passed out.

Since the three of us who weren't horizontal had difficulty walking, it was no easy task to wake up the other guys. It was even harder to get home because the guy who hit the tree needed support, and Ron and I had to practically carry Mitch to his house, where we dropped him onto his front lawn and ran away.

I found out later he'd been taken to the hospital to get his stomach pumped.

Somehow, I managed to get home, where I promptly threw up several times in the bathroom— some of it even made it into the toilet. At first, my mom and dad thought I'd caught some kind of bug. I could tell my older brother wasn't buying that.

It certainly didn't smell like a bug.

It also didn't help that after Mitch sobered up, he ratted us all out, and his parents called our families to pass on the news.

Therapy Session cont.

Ursula frowned. "That's quite a story," she commented.

"Sorry about the crudeness," I said, realizing just how out of control we'd been, especially for a bunch of sixth graders. "But, that's how it happened."

"No need to apologize," she assured me. "Did you get in much trouble with your parents after the party at the lake?"

"Not really." I shrugged. "Fortunately, my older brother had paved the way. My folks weren't overly shocked. A little surprised, maybe. I was the good kid for the most part."

"We'll definitely spend some time talking about your family history," Ursula commented. "But, back to the alcohol. Did you do more heavy drinking after the lake incident?"

"Do you mean ever? Or just as a kid?" I could feel my cheeks heating up. It was embarrassing to admit to some of my past behavior. "My college days were pretty intense as far as drugs and alcohol."

"Let's stick with high school at this point."

"It wasn't like we binged every weekend," I said. "But, I do recall drinking most of a jug of cheap white wine in seventh grade, and a whole six-pack of malt liquor in ninth grade."

"That's a lot of alcohol," Ursula remarked. "Especially for such a young brain. You've probably heard the term 'neuroplasticity' in all your recovery work."

"I have," I said. "It's basically the brain's ability to create new neural pathways, right?"

"That's it in a nutshell," she agreed. "Our brains are very flexible. You probably have some limitations, mostly from so many years of opioids, but you can still learn new skills."

"Retrain the brain," I said.

"Exactly. And, it's best to learn new things that use both hemispheres of the brain. Like music or a language."

"Or juggling," I said. "I've been working on that one."

"Or juggling." She chuckled. "Or, in your case, writing about addiction and recovery. Everyone should be doing something to build up the brain as they age. I know I need it more and more."

"Really?" I asked, intrigued by the personal revelation. "What kind of stuff do you do?"

It was Ursula's turn to earn a little color in her cheeks. For a moment, I thought I may have stepped over the doctor/patient line.

"I paint," she said, gesturing to different pieces around her office. "I'm not a great artist. I just look at a photo and replicate it."

I looked at all the Southwest desert artwork on her walls. "I thought most of those were photographs."

"No," she replied. "Those are all my paintings. I mostly copied them from photographs." She folded her hands in her lap. "I don't have the talent to create it from scratch."

I smiled. It sure looked like she had plenty of talent to me.

Survival Tips

The problem with brain development, especially during childhood, is that by the time you are in trouble, it's too late. The damage is done.

The human brain isn't fully developed until our mid-to-late twenties. Think about what that means for the eighteen-year-old soldier who must kill to survive combat, or the twelve-year-old child who is repeatedly molested by a family member.

The good news is that you can get your brain back into shape. And, you can do so by getting passionate about something in your life. These survival tips are focused on picking up new skills or abilities that give the brain a workout, especially when both analytical and creative parts of the brain are engaged.

Music: Learning to read music and play an instrument improves concentration, focus, and memory. It also helps develop physical coordination and movement. Even listening to music can increase neuroplasticity, as well as relieve stress.

Art: Art therapy is very popular in rehab centers. It can open up new perspectives and help patients express insights or personal challenges that are difficult to put into words. Art enhances creativity and can be very relaxing. It can even be used as a technique for surfing urges and cravings. I had a friend in rehab who would doodle on a pad during group sessions. It was her way of dealing with the stressful topics that came up.

Exercise: Obviously, movement and exercise keep our bodies fit and healthy. Brain connectivity can also be increased through exercise, particularly when learning something new. Practicing movements builds new neural pathways that can improve cognitive ability. And, it doesn't have to be something as hardcore as running a marathon. It doesn't even have to be a new skill. I used to juggle back in college and have taken it up again as a way to work on mental concentration (and have fun).

Language: Learning an entirely new language is an incredible workout for the brain. Cognitive functioning, attention span, and memory improve as the brain makes those new connections.

Games: Checkers, Chess, Risk, and other board games all involve problem solving, memory, creative thinking, visual recognition, and reaction time. It doesn't have to be a board game if that's not your thing. Video games get a bad rap, but they are convenient, easy to use, and can support neuroplasticity. As an official member of AARP, I can tell you that their experts highly recommend video games to improve and maintain brain health. Other brain builders include puzzles and word games.

Our brains have amazing resilience. I met a friend in rehab who, two years prior, had brain damage from an injury that reduced his cognitive skills to those of a second grader. By the time I met him, he had retrained his brain and was functioning at the level he'd been at before the injury.

Anything that uses both creativity and analytical prowess is destined to help create those new, healthy neural pathways. Even a basic project, such as building a shelf, uses long-term conceptual planning, as well as skills that require paying attention to detail. Planning and planting a garden is another project that develops the intellect, and it's a great way to connect to nature—and to grow good food.

The brain, like the body, needs exercise and rest.

Use it or lose it.

CHAPTER
FOUR
STORED TRAUMA

Therapy Session

"Let's talk about your family," Ursula encouraged. "You lived with your mom and dad, so you weren't raised by a single parent. You were the youngest, and Mark, your brother, was three years older. Your paperwork lists another brother, Craig, who was sixteen years older than you. That's quite a gap."

I was in my usual overstuffed chair, sitting across from her. "Craig was my hero," I said. "He was more of a dad to me than my father."

"Your history states that Craig died of cancer several years ago." She jotted down some notes on her ever-present legal pad.

I felt the pull of sadness that always assailed me whenever I thought of Craig, and I sank lower into my seat cushion. It was a sense of longing, tinged with regret, that such a great and kind man had been taken too early from this world.

"My folks had Craig during WWII when a lot of babies were conceived before the dads left for the war. I guess my parents decided to wait a while for more kids."

Ursula sat up straight, smoothed out her gray skirt, and gave her black blazer a downward tug. It dawned on me that she sat up like that whenever I started slouching down in my chair.

"So, you were the youngest," she said. "What role did you play in your family?"

I sat up and squared my shoulders. "As you've heard, I was no angel. But, I still played the role of the good kid who tried to please my folks," I replied. "I think I also was the 'hero' in the sense that I was so good at sports and excelled at everything I did once I reached high school and college."

"During our first session, you said your dad was emotionally unavailable. What did you mean by that?"

I balled up my fists, then immediately made my hands relax—but it was too late. My ever-vigilant therapist noticed and made another note.

"To sum up our relationship, he only came to one of my ball games," I said. "I know that sounds like whining, but you gotta understand. I was involved in hundreds and hundreds of baseball games, football games, track meets, and so on. And, I was often the best athlete on the team." I clenched my jaw. "I mean, why even have kids if you're not going to spend time with them?"

"I think we've dug up some old trauma," Ursula observed. "That's good."

"I remember not that many years ago when my dad was still alive, I'd dropped by to see him. I made the mistake of asking him what dreams he'd had as a young man."

"Why was that a mistake?"

"He said he always wanted to be a bush pilot up in Alaska," I answered. "I never knew that about him. He'd retired from a career as a personnel manager for a medical insurance outfit in San Francisco. Not something most folks aspire to. Then, he said that he had kids, and it ruined his dream."

"What did you say to that?" she asked.

"Actually, I didn't say a thing, but I remember thinking, *hey, Dad, I'm sitting right in front of you. I'm one of those kids who ruined your dreams.*"

Ursula grimaced. "I bet that stung. Those kinds of emotional jolts get stuck in the body until you deal with them."

My anger started to fade and was replaced with a twinge of shame for bashing my dad. I looked out the big window of Ursula's office to collect my thoughts. The glass was so old that the ripples made the landscape outside look like it was underwater. I liked having a view of the historic downtown. It kept me connected to the outside world.

"What are you thinking?" Ursula asked.

"I was just thinking about how my dad probably

did the best he could for what he knew about parenting. I was never abused, always had plenty to eat, and had a nice place to live."

"And he didn't?"

"He adored his mom, Mabel," I answered. "She was the only grandparent I met. The others passed away before I was born. I know that his dad, Lyle, was a drunk and died in a gutter."

"Yikes. Was your dad's father living with the family when he died?"

"Not at that point. Lyle was an out-of-work mason living on the street. The only story my dad shared was about the night his old man showed up drunk at the door of their upstairs apartment. Lyle forced his way in and hit Mabel. My dad was the oldest kid, about twelve, and had a younger brother and sister. He ended up shoving my grandpa down the stairs. A couple of months later, Lyle was found dead on the street from alcohol poisoning."

"Clearly, your dad didn't have healthy male role-modeling in his life," Ursula commented. "I'm sure you're right that he did the best he could, but his lack of connecting with you as a child is a part of what shaped your values and beliefs about the world. What about your mom's upbringing?"

"You know, it just hit me that my mom didn't come to my ball games either. I never held that against her, though. That's strange," I said. "But, she had her traumas too."

"Like what?"

"My mother was abandoned by her father when she was just a baby. The story I was told was that her mother, Gladys, became severely depressed. At one point, Grandma Gladys had my mom in her arms and walked onto a high bridge over a shallow river. She intended to jump and take my mom with her."

"I take it that didn't happen since you're here to tell the story," Ursula remarked.

"No, but Gladys was unfit to care for anyone, and my mom was placed in a Catholic boarding school where she stayed for several years."

"So, you do have some family history of substance abuse and depression," Ursula summed up. "Genetics also plays a role in emotional development."

I furrowed my brows and crossed my arms. Anger seemed to be my emotion of the day. "Then, why didn't my brothers suffer from depression like I did? What happened to me that didn't happen to them?"

"It's just not as simple as that," Ursula said carefully. "Everyone's brain is wired differently. It seems like both you and your brother, Mark, didn't get much approval or praise from your father. In a way, Mark's rebellious nature was a healthier response than your need to please your dad. He had a sort of outlet, while you hid your feelings under the surface. Stuffed it down."

"He certainly got more attention than I did, but it wasn't very positive."

"Exactly," she said. "I'm sure it wasn't very pleasant for your brother being the one who caught more of the heat. But it was still attention. All kids need a sense of connection and belonging to their family, especially their parents."

"My parents thought I was pretty squared away and could take care of myself," I said. "And, there's some truth to that."

"To a point," Ursula countered. "But, you were still a kid. Your brain was far from developed, and those experiences stuck. How did your parents' divorce impact your life?"

I sighed. "Like a ton of bricks."

———

I was surprised when Tina took me by the hand, walked me into her bedroom, and then stripped off all her clothes. I had just moved from California to Wyoming, and this was my first real date with her. We both worked at the local pizza parlor. I was seventeen and had just started my senior year in high school.

My parents had recently divorced. So, my mom and I moved to Jackson Hole, where my eldest brother lived. Mom was a mess; Dad had been screwing some younger women, and I guess it came as a bit of a shock to her.

It was news to me too.

Now, here I was in a cozy little log cabin, complete with a crackling fire and Tina, who was nineteen, an older woman. I'd only known her for a month. She'd been engaged, but her fiancé was killed in a car crash a few months earlier while driving from the East Coast to join her in Wyoming.

Even though I was taken aback by how fast things were moving, I had the wherewithal to shed my clothes and join her in bed. It was amazing. All my previous sexual encounters had either been awkward tumbles in a car or sneaking off to the woods to fumble around in the dark. And, not only was I in an actual bed, but I spent the entire night. Both firsts for me.

If this were adulthood, then I was all for it.

Technically, I wasn't yet an adult. I was still a couple of months shy of my eighteenth birthday and was a new student at Jackson Hole High School. My mom had rented an apartment not far from my brother's place. She was a basket case and started drinking a lot more than usual.

I was a little dismayed at the move from California to Wyoming. It felt like I'd been ripped out of my former "normal" life. All my closest friends, as well as a budding romance, had been suddenly left behind. But I had not only agreed to make the move so Mom would have some family support—I even suggested it. I could've stayed at my friend Jack's house to finish my senior year, but I chose not to. It was one of the biggest mistakes I ever made.

However, my night with Tina made things a lot more bearable. Little did I know that this was just the beginning. A week later, I moved into an old, red and white, single-wide trailer with Tina for the rest of my senior year.

Mom didn't seem to mind.

Therapy Session cont.

"Like I said, that's a lot of loss for a 17-year-old," Ursula mused. "It sounds like you and your mother swapped roles."

"I guess I never really thought about it as a loss. More like just growing up real fast," I said. "What do you mean by swapping roles?"

"In effect, you became the parent to your mother, and she became the one who had to be cared for," Ursula explained. "You sacrificed staying at the high school in the community in which you were raised. You sacrificed relationships with your closest friends, including the 'budding romance' you mentioned. Those things are huge to a teenager."

She was right. I'd pretty much stuffed away all those feelings decades ago, but if I was honest with myself, I still had some resentment floating around in the back of my mind.

"But, she really needed me." I shrugged.

"It wasn't your job. You were a kid," Ursula replied. "I imagine you didn't know how to grieve, or even know it was grief that you were experiencing. Think about it. You lost your friends. You lost your ability to play the sports you loved and were so accomplished at. Through the divorce—which sounds like it blindsided you—you lost your dad and, for all intents and purposes, lost who your mom used to be."

"You're right about being blindsided," I agreed. "My folks had been married for 35 years. Who gets divorced after that long? I thought they were happy together until the very end."

"How did you find out about the divorce?"

I snorted. "On the longest car ride of my life. It was the summer between my junior and senior years of high school. Before I lived with Tina in that trailer. I'd spent July and August working in Wyoming and living at my brother's house. My parents came from California to pick me up." I paused for a moment, lost in the memory.

"I remember they were awfully quiet and subdued on the ride," I continued. "Then, about halfway through the barren salt flats of Utah, it was, 'Oh, by the way, son, your mom and I are getting divorced.' Let's just say it was a very uncomfortable thousand miles after that."

"There are definitely some themes that have developed in your life. I'd say they started with that attack by the kid with the spiked board," Ursula commented. "As we discussed, abandonment was clearly one of them."

Ursula sat back in her chair and steepled her fingers. "Many of your traumatic experiences were never really resolved. And speaking of resolving stored trauma, I saw in your background paperwork that you've done a lot of Eye Movement Desensitization and Reprocessing therapy."

"I have. For me, EMDR was a lot like the Somatic Experiencing. It really helped clear up some old stuff.

Survival Tips

Eye Movement Desensitization and Reprocessing: EMDR was critical to my recovery. Like any other therapy, it's the relationship with the practitioner that matters most.

During sessions, my therapist would target specific traumatic or disturbing memories in my life. They could be emotions, thoughts, or physical sensations. For example, when I lost my career to opioid addiction, I was severely traumatized. It was all I could think about, and the shame and anger were overwhelming. My therapist would have me focus on that memory. Then he'd asked me, on a 1 to 10 scale (ten being the worst), how I scored that memory. At the beginning of the session, that number was ten. Then he would use EMDR (this particular therapist used a horizontal light bar) to process the memory on both sides (hemispheres) of my brain. After using the stimulation, he once again asked me to score the trauma on a scale of 1 to 10. Inevitably, the numbers would go down. He would repeat the process until we got the score down to about 3.

EMDR can be as simple as following a therapist's finger back and forth with your eyes while discussing a traumatic event. Other techniques might include the therapist tapping your knee, using audio stimulation through headphones, or using the horizontal light bar mentioned above for tracking eye movement.

While doing bilateral stimulation activity (like following the therapist's finger back and forth), the client engages with their traumatic memory, changing the way the patient thinks and feels about it.

Although EMDR sessions are most effective when conducted by certified therapists, there are a couple of techniques you can do at home that are based on the EMDR model of stimulating both hemispheres of the brain.

Knee Tapping: Sit in a comfortable chair with both feet flat on the floor. Begin the four-count breathing we learned in Chapter One. Place both hands, palms down, on your knees. Using your fingertips, take turns tapping one knee and then the other.

Shoulder/Forearm Tapping: Sit in a comfortable chair. Settle back in the chair and begin four-count breathing. Cross your arms over your chest and place your hands, palms down, on your forearms. Alternate tapping your forearms with your hands. If you can reach, place your palms down on your upper arms and begin tapping.

The ultimate goal of EMDR is to get traumas unstuck so that the neural healing of your mind and body can move forward. I think of it like a cut on my hand. The ability of my body to heal that cut is nothing short of miraculous. But if I keep irritating the wound and causing it to re-open, it's not going to heal very fast. In fact, it could become infected.

CHAPTER
FIVE
DORM DAZE

Therapy Session

I took a seat in what I now thought of as *my* chair and looked around Ursula's office. The early autumn sun streamed through the big, rippled window and infused the old brick walls with a mellow glow.

I thought back on a number of cold, windowless offices where I'd received therapy over the years. The kind of rooms lit by buzzing fluorescent lights with posters on the wall that screamed SUCCESS, TEAMWORK, or PERSEVERANCE. Posters that boasted ultra-fit people running marathons or climbing cliffs, or other things that are unattainable for mere mortals like me.

Ursula's fingers were steepled again. "What are you thinking about, Scott?"

"I was thinking how comfortable it feels here."

She smiled. "Well, that's good." Once again, her

office was adorned with freshly cut flowers. This time it was sunflowers, petals golden in the light. "I was going over some of the events that shaped your life. Many of them were out of your control."

I said nothing.

"I know it sounds a little over-simplified," she said. "But, the whole thing about your dad only coming to one ball game speaks volumes. You spent years hoping for attention and praise that never came. That's one reason you've been so driven to succeed. In a sense, even though your father is dead, you're still seeking that recognition."

I felt my body tense. She was treading into dangerous territory.

"I'd never been close to my dad," I said. "But, after my folks divorced, our relationship became barely civil."

"Nevertheless, he was still your dad."

I instinctively reached for the bracelets on my left wrist and gave them a few tugs. They were on strong, elastic cords strung with small, polished stones of various colors. They were a gift from my wife.

"I was always pretty focused on having to be number one, especially during my career. I just never thought of it as being a daddy issue. It's kind of pathetic."

"It's all too common. Especially among men," Ursula replied. "Let's shift gears. We've covered up through high school. Now, tell me about your college days. I'd like to focus on drug use, but it doesn't have to be limited to that."

———

I don't know whose idea it was, but I was the one who kicked in the sauna door. The Quaaludes and alcohol we'd consumed might have had something to do with it.

"Whoa, I didn't think you could do it," said Mike. "I'm impressed."

"Man, that was loud," Steve said, glancing around nervously. "I'll bet somebody's going to call the campus cops." Steve was the most cautious of our foursome, the only one who'd voiced some concerns about our little caper before we were too wasted to care.

"No one heard it, you wuss," Tom sneered. He was the most intense and reckless of the group. He even made me look tame. The only reason Tom didn't do the door kicking was that I was the biggest guy. It was my sophomore year at California State University, Sacramento. We were all living on the same dormitory floor and had become fast friends.

We'd been partying in Tom's room since early evening and decided that using the sauna in the basement of our dorm building would be a good idea. Unfortunately, time had gotten away from us, and the sauna door had been locked since 10:00 PM.

"Someone's going to bust us," Steve worried. "Maybe we should get the hell out of here."

"No one is down here this late," Tom declared, shedding his clothes. "Come on, it'll be fine."

The rest of us stripped down and piled into the

cedar-lined sauna, which was kept running at all times and was plenty hot. I grabbed a wooden bucket of water from the floor and poured it on the rocks that topped the heating element. It gave off a satisfying sizzle, and the room filled with eucalyptus-scented steam. Tom turned off the light, and we sprawled out on the double deck of benches. Each of us became lost in our own altered state.

The evening had started like many others. For us, partying trumped academics, and we began with a card game called Warm-Up. If you drew a certain card, you had to either drink a six-ounce glass of beer, down a shot of whiskey, or take a hit off the bong.

It didn't take us long to lose our judgment.

Then, Tom magically produced a small plastic bag containing a bunch of capsules. They were Quaaludes, a brand-new experience for me. We popped a few and the next thing we knew, we were on our way to the sauna.

I was enjoying the heat but noticed that the "ludes" were really kicking in much stronger than I thought they'd be. My body felt like it was made of rubber, and I imagined myself slowly melting into the cedar bench. It was pitch dark, and I couldn't see the others.

Then, I heard Tom's disembodied voice. "It's too hot," he said.

I heard moist wood creaking, followed by a loud crash. I groped for the light and turned it on. Tom was lying on the floor, gripping his right arm. I smelled burning flesh.

"Are you okay?" Mike worried.

"I don't know," Tom groaned.

"Let me see," I said, and he held out his arm. I cringed as, right before my eyes, a large grid-shaped burn started to grow and blister on Tom's entire forearm. The wound matched the metal grid covering the hot rocks on the heating element.

"It was getting too hot, and I was going to turn it down," said Tom. "But when I stood up, I lost my balance and fell. I landed right on top of the fucking heater."

"That looks horrible," Steve remarked. "I bet it hurts like hell."

Tom looked at the damage and grinned wistfully. "Actually, I don't feel it at all."

"Good thing it wasn't your face," Mike commented.

"Yeah, good thing," I said, thinking it was the adrenaline and drugs keeping the pain at bay. It was a brutal burn, so he was going to be hurting soon. "We need to get out of here and get that looked at."

We threw on our clothes and headed back to the dorm. Steve woke up one of the resident assistants, who was trained in first aid and had a kit handy. We told him what happened. I guess he kept it to himself because we never suffered any consequences.

Except for Tom. He still carries that grid of scars.

Therapy Session cont.

"Quaaludes," Ursula repeated. "I haven't heard that word in years."

"They went out of fashion a long time ago," I said. "Probably a good thing."

"What other drugs did you experience in college?"

"It's easier to say which ones I didn't do," I replied. I felt a rush of shame creep up my cheeks. "I never did heroin or PCP, but I did have a couple more surgeries and trips to the hospital, and that meant more opioids. Those were dark days for me."

"What do you think the darkness was about?"

"My folks' divorce," I answered and gave one of my elastic bracelets a snap. "It took a while, but it hit me pretty hard."

"You were nineteen during those hospital stays, right?" Ursula clarified. "Did either of your parents visit you in the hospital?"

"No, they didn't. But my mom was living in Wyoming at the time."

"What about your dad?" she asked.

Tears immediately welled in my eyes. I took a deep breath.

"He lived about half an hour away, with his new girlfriend." I broke eye contact with Ursula, hunched forward, and stared at the floor. Ursula leaned forward in her chair, closing the gap between our knees to a couple of inches, but she remained quiet.

I took a swipe at my damp eyes with the back of my hand.

"I always thought that the serious, suicidal depression didn't start until I lost my career in my forties," I said. "But, I remember driving down the freeway one day during my college days. I had this overwhelming urge to slam my Mustang into a cement column that supported an overpass."

"But, you're here now," Ursula said gently. "And, it sounds like when you went to the college dorms, drug use aside, you made a lot of good connections and friends."

I looked up. "That's true. Things started to get a lot better for me. I had a ton of close friends and a steady girlfriend."

"I assume the sauna incident wasn't your only reckless adventure,"

"Not even close."

"I think I've got a pretty good handle on the college days," Ursula said. "And, we're out of time anyway. Next session, let's dig into your career in law enforcement."

Survival Tips

Bracelets: Using bracelets as a distraction is a technique I learned in recovery that helps with getting through urges to take drugs, slip into depression, or spin off into a panic attack. Pulling and snapping the bracelet is my standard go-to if I start to get anxious, frustrated, or even angry. After all the medical trauma I suffered, even waiting in a doctor's office can trigger me. The sensation of the beads gently hitting the inside of my wrist is calming for me. Silently counting out each bead is another low-key distraction technique.

Some bracelets have lava stones meant to absorb essential oils like those mentioned in Chapter Two. Just dab a little on and it lasts most of the day. Some bracelets may have crystals, magnets, or pressure-point beads. I've never tried them, but I once asked a more open-minded doctor about using non-Western modes of healing. She said, "If they work, what does it matter?" And that was good enough for me.

I look at snapping bracelets as a helpful tool on my recovery tool belt. If people want to upgrade to the Cadillac bracelets, I'm all for it. As I sit here and write this book, I have two bracelets on my left wrist. They are made of a strong elastic cord strung with several stone beads, including some lava stone meant to absorb essential oils. A large rubber band or my wife's hair ties work in a pinch.

When shopping online, look for an anti-anxiety bracelet or therapy bracelet.

Yellow Bracelet: While I was at a reunion for one of my rehab stints, they were giving out green and yellow rubber wristbands. If you chose to wear the green one, it meant it was okay to approach and talk to that person. The yellow bracelet meant "caution, do not approach without consent". At first, I thought it was a little silly.

However, when I got home, I found it to be an

excellent tool for communicating my mood to my wife. I use the yellow bracelet sparingly, and my wife knows not to engage during those times. It's also a good reminder for me to notice my mood and take it easy.

PART TWO

The Downward Spiral

CHAPTER
SIX
ADRENALINE JUNKIE

Therapy Session

"You look upset," Ursula observed. "Is everything okay?"

I sat up straight in my chair and rolled my shoulders. "I'm fine," I said. "On my way over here, I was mulling over a few things that bugged me."

"Such as?"

"During my many months of rehab, there were always counselors who insisted that people turn to drugs because their lives suck."

Ursula ran a hand through her hair. It was longer than when we first met, and it suited her. "You don't think that's the case with you?"

"I get that some people use drugs to escape bad situations like abuse or poverty," I said. "And, that they'd finally found something that made them feel good, but, overall, I had a pretty decent life."

Ursula was quiet for a moment.

"You've never felt like you needed to escape from something or that you were running from anything in your life?" she asked, one eyebrow raised.

I crossed my arms. "Not really. I always thought about drugs and alcohol as part of partying and having fun. Not as something I needed because I felt bad about myself or wanted to escape."

Ursula took a long, slow breath and let it out. "How about to stave off depression or anxiety?" she asked. "Or to deaden chronic, physical pain? Or to deal with the trauma of what you saw as a cop?"

She had a point there.

"I guess I was mostly thinking about my younger days."

"You weren't suffering the negative impacts of addiction during your younger days," said Ursula. "You took risks and were introduced to a lot of alcohol and drug use during your tender years. Lots of kids have those experiences. What I'm trying to get at is this: you didn't become an addict until much later in life."

Addict. I flinched at the word. I'd grown used to the label and had even accepted it to a point, but it still stung to hear the word out loud.

"Are you saying that someone else could've gone through life exactly as I did and not get addicted?"

"It's not as simple as that," she said, "but the answer is yes, at least to begin with. No one experiences things exactly the same way. When you add in genetics, family history, your career choice, and all the opioids that accompanied your injuries and surgeries, the odds of addiction increase."

I closed my eyes and said nothing. We let the silence drift for a while. It was a comfortable silence. Safe.

Ursula decided to change the subject.

"We've talked about how trauma gets stored in the body. Tell me some of your traumatic experiences as a police officer."

———

I knew when the guy kicked my partner, Anna, in the head, it wasn't going to be pretty.

I'd been a cop in the San Francisco Bay Area for about a year and had already experienced a lot of fights, but this guy was different. He was huge, like Schwarzenegger in his glory days. And, judging by the skill it took to perform a perfectly executed roundhouse kick to my partner's head, this guy knew how to fight.

Anna and I had been dispatched to a call of a man beating up a woman in the parking lot of a local hotel. Sure enough, upon arrival, we saw the mountain of muscle punching a local hooker named Misty in the face. Anna yelled at the guy to stop, but then got too close. That's when the kick to the head came, and my partner was knocked out cold.

My first thought was to draw my gun and order the guy to the ground, but I knew he wouldn't. I didn't want to kill the guy. I just wanted to stop him.

The attacker dropped into a fighting stance with his ham-like fists out in front of him. Knowing he could crumple me with one punch, I drew my baton. Using both hands, I swung with all my strength and heard the baton impact one of his fists like a bat hitting a side of beef.

To my amazement, he just drew his hand back and looked at it for a split second, then got back into his stance. I'd found out later from the paramedics that my blow had shattered several bones in the guy's hand, but you wouldn't know it by looking at him at the time.

Anna came to and staggered to her feet to join the fray. For what seemed like hours—but was really just a few seconds—it was a battle of the two of us swinging our batons, and the suspect throwing punches and kicks. Nobody was winning.

The sweet sound of sirens finally erupted in the distance. The cavalry was on its way.

Anna got a little too close again, and the guy tackled her, wrapped a giant forearm around her neck, and began to squeeze. I dove in and repeatedly slammed the end of my baton into the attacker's ribs. He took his other arm and grabbed for my crotch. I twisted at the last second, and he latched onto my inner thigh like a vice. The resulting bruise was about the size of a dinner plate. Fueled by adrenaline, I continued to hammer his ribs until he finally loosened his grip on both of us.

We discarded our batons, and each grabbed one of the guy's massive arms in an effort to get him into handcuffs. He thrashed around and tried to plant his feet. He was able to swing both of us back and forth like we were little kids wrestling our dad.

Several patrol cars came screaming into the parking lot. It wasn't until we had the weight of six guys on the attacker that we were able to finally get him under control.

I found out later that he was wanted for murder.

Therapy Session cont.

"How was the hooker?" Ursula asked.

"She went to the hospital," I replied. "But, she was back on the streets the following week."

"Pretty brutal stuff."

"It's a brutal world." I shifted around in my chair. It'd been a while since I'd shared a cop story. I'd sliced off that whole part of my life.

"I'd imagine that story is just the tip of the iceberg as far as being exposed to violence," Ursula commented. "How did you deal with all the stress at the end of the day?"

"Day? I didn't see much daylight for several years. I mostly worked the graveyard shift with a few swing shifts. That's where the action was. We all dealt with the stress by drinking. There was even a cop bar that was open all the time, so all the shifts could use it. I remember how weird it was to go to a bar at eight in the morning and wander out into the sunlight just before lunch."

I started tapping my foot on the rug. The urge to get up and move was overwhelming.

Ursula noticed.

"I was thinking back to when you asked the big 'why me' question regarding your opioid addiction," she said. "Your career choice was rife with unhealthy circumstances. It's been proven time and again that humans are not designed for working all night and sleeping during the day. It's also extremely abnormal to run toward gunfire instead of running away from it. You literally have to override the part of your brain that's screaming at you to flee."

"You've got a good grip on the realities of the job." I smiled grimly.

"My brother was a police officer," she revealed. "I know it's rare to have a positive encounter when you work in law enforcement. Even the victims, who may be thankful for your help, aren't thinking about that during an emergency situation."

I dropped my guard a bit. Most people have no clue about what it's like to be a cop. I narrowed my eyes and stared off into space.

"What are you thinking, Scott?"

"I was thinking how you never really asked me the details on how I lost my job."

"Tell me what happened," she replied.

"Basically, I retired on a *non-duty-related* medical retirement, which, unfortunately, gives me a fraction of the income that a *duty*-related medical retirement would've provided."

Ursula's brows rose. "They didn't consider all those on-duty injuries job-related?"

"Nope," I replied, cringing at the bitterness in my voice. "Not back then. I wasn't forced from my job by the city council or anything. I wasn't fired or politely asked to leave. I quit because I could no longer do my job with all the pain and fatigue."

I couldn't seem to keep my foot still, but plowed on anyway. "It was complicated. Back then, I had no idea it was the opioids, and I was diagnosed with things like fibromyalgia, Lyme disease, and untreatable Major Depressive Disorder. Not a single doctor told me that it might be the pain meds."

"Sometimes specialists have a narrow focus," Ursula observed. "It's like that saying, 'to a hammer, everything looks like a nail'."

I snorted. "True. My rheumatologist was convinced it was lupus, and one of my psychiatrists diagnosed my muddled thinking as Executive Function Disorder. Anyway, I had several more surgeries for the pain, and, of course, more meds. Then, the stress of a major lawsuit put another heavy rock in my backpack, and I completely broke down."

Now, my foot was tapping at hyper-speed, and I could feel my heart starting to pound in my chest like a bass drum.

Ursula set down her notepad and stood up. "I've got an idea," she said. "It's a beautiful autumn day.

Would you like to get out of the office for a few minutes? Maybe take a walk along the creek trail. I think it would really help if you moved around a little."

"You mean right now?"

"Why not?" She walked over to the large window and peered out. "I read that you are into qigong and yoga. Maybe we could try a few moves down by the creek?"

"I don't move very well these days," I said, as I stood up, "but it would be nice to get outdoors."

I was a little embarrassed. Then again, I'm a guy who's wandered down the hallway of a psych ward wearing nothing but a backless hospital gown, so a little qigong out in public with my counselor sounded doable.

We headed out down the old rickety wooden stairs and onto the street. The creek trail was a heavily treed green space that stretched for several blocks parallel to the old downtown district. It was a typical, sunny day in New Mexico, and we soon arrived at a small lawn area with a couple of benches overlooking the creek. The tall cottonwoods were clad in their golden fall leaves, and the midday sun sparkled on the water like a thousand tiny diamonds.

I'd done my routines outdoors many times, so the few spectators wandering the trail didn't bother me. I settled into the qigong stance with my feet hip-width apart, knees slightly bent, and shoulders relaxed.

"Did you have a particular move in mind?" I asked.

Ursula stood next to me and mimicked my stance.

"I don't," she said. "I thought I'd just follow along with you."

I sighed and began a simple routine that I did most days. Qigong had become second nature to me, so I was able to quickly get into the flow, even with my discomfort.

Ursula followed suit.

Survival Tips

Adrenaline is a wonderful thing for a short-term response to a threat. However, humans are not designed for long-term dumping of adrenaline and cortisol hormones into our bodies. These chemicals are great for when a tiger attacks, but not so great for our everyday health.

The human capacity for survival is impressive. When the brain perceives a threat or potential danger, it has a much greater impact on our memories than, say, a pleasant event. The brain stores the threat memory.

Why?

Well, our brains want to remember that deadly threat so the next time we encounter it, we can get a head start on avoiding a tiger attack. It sounds so mechanical, but that's the way it is. Unlike other animals that literally shake off trauma, humans tend to "store it and ignore it."

In this survival tip section, I'll point out a few

relaxation techniques I use to dispel the after-effects of stress and adrenaline. The idea is to work on mindfulness practices that focus on remaining grounded in the present instead of returning to a state of hyperarousal.

One of the best ways to deal with pent-up stress left over from a fight-or-flight event is to get moving. Motion and exercise. As I'll point out in later chapters, motion is one of the few things that can help with surviving opioid withdrawals. Any kind of movement is good, preferably out in nature.

Qigong: What works best for me and my particular challenges is qigong. The myriad forms and styles of qigong can be adapted to almost any disability. Tai chi is an example of the martial form of qigong. Although tai chi is a little more physical, many people get a lot out of it emotionally as well. Qigong directly translates as "energy work."

Yoga: Yoga has been popular for so long that everyone from health providers to professional football trainers uses it to improve the health and performance of their charges. Use caution. It is easy to get cocky and overstretch, which can lead to injury, and some forms of yoga may be too extreme for beginners.

Meditation: The four-count breathing presented in Chapter One is a good example of simple meditation. I see meditation as my mental, emotional, and spiritual in-basket. I am drawing in or absorbing energy. It recharges my battery. There are many techniques for this practice, so find one that works for you.

Prayer/Manifestation: I see prayer as my out-basket. That's when I send all the stuff cluttering up my life out into the universe. I'm not religious in any organized way, but I do think most of the great religions have it right in that they use prayer as a way to open up and let go. If you're uncomfortable with the term prayer, think of it as manifesting. Speaking the good that you want in your life out into the universe.

Immersion: Water pressure is a natural way to calm inflammation, as well as support weak or injured joints and muscles. It has some of the same benefits as a weighted blanket and is also perfect for getting some exercise without over-straining joints and ligaments. Even the steady stream of water from a shower can be helpful.

Walking: It's easy, cheap, accessible, and can be done with other people (and dogs). There are even walking meditations. I've seen folks doing laps in shopping malls, so if the weather is poor, get creative.

I have so many injuries and physical limitations that I stick with qigong, yoga, and some of the mellower forms of mindfulness training, such as meditation and prayer. Some techniques can even be done sitting in a chair.

I try to get out in nature as much as possible. It might be a park or even my own backyard. I think everyone has felt a connection to nature at some point in their lives. Watching the sun slip into the ocean as the sky turns from deep blue to shades of gold and red is mystical, as is walking through an ancient grove of towering redwood trees or spending the night under a moonless desert sky.

CHAPTER
SEVEN
TOXIC ENVIRONMENT

Therapy Session

"Anything come up for you since our last session?" Ursula asked.

"I had a small revelation," I replied. "It's been years since I thought about some of the stuff we've been talking about. Do you remember my story about the guy punching the hooker?"

"Hard to forget."

"Certainly for the hooker."

Since autumn was now in full swing, the usual fresh-cut flowers on Ursula's desk were replaced with a large, woven-straw cornucopia with a dozen tiny pumpkins spilling out.

"The beat I worked most often was the strip where the hookers hung out to practice their trade," I said. "I got to know some of them pretty well, and we got along fine for the most part. I rarely arrested any of them for prostitution. In fact, I usually just gave their customers a citation for soliciting prostitution and left the women alone. I guess I felt sorry for them."

"That makes sense," Ursula replied. "I'm sure it wasn't their first career choice. I would think it takes a lot of desperation to push someone into that line of work."

"Well, every one of them was a heroin addict," I continued. "It was a crime in California to simply be under the influence of heroin. I'd arrest them for that and bring them to the station for processing. They were almost always lucid and cooperative, and I was even on a first-name basis with some of them."

I looked out the window, struggling to frame my thoughts. "Looking back, I realize they were going through the same thing I went through years later as an opioid addict."

Ursula nodded. "That's good. Go on."

"When I brought them to the station, I'd have them take a urine test for heroin, and then I had the option of booking them into jail or releasing them on a written promise to appear in court. I remember they were always so desperate to get released. Even though jail sucks, I thought their fear was out of proportion. At least they'd have a place to sleep and get a few decent meals."

"They didn't want to go through heroin withdrawals," Ursula said.

Man, she was good.

"Bingo. They say opioid withdrawals don't kill

you, but you'll wish they did. In my experience, truer words have never been spoken."

"So, you've learned some compassion and empathy for others. That's a good thing."

"And a whole lot of humility," I said. "I'm actually looking into signing up for a week-long course to become a certified peer support counselor to help other opioid addicts. I would have done anything to avoid those withdrawals. Anything it took, and I did. I was just lucky enough to have more resources than some people."

"That sounds like something we can address in more detail later," Ursula said carefully. "I would caution you about jumping into peer support at this point in your recovery, but first, I'd like to hear more about your move out of the Bay Area. You stayed in law enforcement, so I assume the traumatic experiences kept coming."

———

The guy was in jail for beating his mother to death with a hammer. With his shaved head, thickly muscled body, and soulless eyes, I thought he looked the part. Of course, nobody looked very good in a bright orange jumpsuit.

I was a deputy sheriff in the Sierra Nevada foothills and was working the floor at the county jail. I hated it. My wife and I had just moved to the mountains, and I started out assigned to patrol— similar to my last job. But then, I was reassigned to the jail, and that was a whole new world. Working the floor for twelve hours a day was excruciatingly boring; all I did was play nursemaid to a slew of inmates. A glorified babysitter. It got to the point that I preferred working in the booking room where the street cops brought in drunks and violent criminals.

I'd been watching the mom-killer the past few days, and something seemed off. He was in the smaller of the jail's "pods" along with the other killers who were awaiting trial. Usually, he was sullen and rarely made eye contact, but recently, he was almost friendly.

It bothered me enough that I checked the court schedule and noticed he was slated to be transported to the county courthouse the next day for a hearing. That meant that a deputy would pick him up, handcuff him, and transport him a couple of miles to court.

I decided to search his cell. Something we did now and then. What we usually found was a nasty concoction called Pruno. The inmates would save up fruit juice, or what passed for fruit juice in that place, and sneak some bread. Then, they'd put the bread in with the juice and let the yeast and sugar do their thing. The result was alcohol.

Desperate measures.

The killer was in the dayroom that he shared with his peers, sitting on a steel stool bolted to the floor, at a steel table, also bolted to the floor. I told him to stay put while I searched his private room. I could see his whole body tense up, his eyes shifting back and forth.

I started looking in the usual places: under the thin, plastic mattress on the steel shelf that served as a bed; behind the steel, lidless toilet. Then, I stood on the bed and examined the small, metal grate that covered the ventilation duct. I saw what looked like a white thread tied to the grate and slowly pulled on it. It was dental floss, and there was something heavier tied to the other end.

With a final tug of the floss, I pulled out a narrow, four-inch blade—a shiv—with tape wrapped around one end for a handle.

But, there was something else.

I pulled out some more floss. Tied to the end was a handcuff key.

The mom-killer wasn't very happy. The deputy who'd been assigned to transport the inmate to court the next day, however, was very happy. In fact, he bought me a six-pack of beer, which was much better than Pruno.

Therapy Session cont.

"That's just plain sinister," Ursula remarked.

"It was a toxic place to work," I replied. "On the streets, at least now and then, I could get away from all the negative vibes. In the jail, someone was always cutting their wrists, hanging themselves, trying to escape, or raping some weaker guy."

"Not very good for your mental health."

"No. I remember one time coming home and putting my fist through a wall. And it was just because I'd had a long day."

I wasn't surprised when Ursula jotted something down on her pad.

"You'd mentioned previously that drinking alcohol was how you dealt with stress in your job," she said. "Was that still the case while you were in the Sierras?"

"Absolutely. I started to drink more. It was the first time I remember thinking of it as a habit instead of just relaxing."

"So, you felt you drank too much?"

"I did." I nodded. "No one was bugging me about it, not even my wife. It wasn't like I was coming into work under the influence, but I felt it was starting to get out of control."

"How about pain relievers?" Ursula asked. "Did you have any injuries or surgeries during your first few years on the job where you were prescribed opioids?"

"Oh, yeah," I replied. "I started getting intense back pain even during my first year in the Bay Area. I tried all kinds of physical therapy and went to a chiropractor, but it didn't help. A doctor finally ended up prescribing opioids—and it helped somewhat." I put my hands over my face and slowly exhaled.

Ursula wisely changed the topic. "How long did you work in the jail?"

"Just a year." I lowered my hands into my lap. "Like I said, I couldn't stand it. I applied for a position at one of the city police departments in that county. It was a good move. I was back working the streets, which I loved, and spent a good chunk of my career with that agency."

"So, no more punching walls?" Ursula asked.

I smiled. "Nope. No more wall punching."

Survival Tips

I remember an old joke where a guy tells his doctor that every time he drinks iced tea, he gets a sharp pain in his left eye. The doctor replies, "Well, then take out the spoon."

While going through residential recovery, I met a lot of addicts who, once they left rehab, headed straight back to the same destructive relationships and environments that fostered the problem in the first place. The result was either another trip to rehab—or a trip to the morgue. That wasn't the case for me. My wife was the rock that kept me alive and gave me enough hope and support to crawl forward on my road to recovery. Most of my family and friends were, and still are, supportive.

Toxic People: We all know a toxic person or two. They're the ones that suck all the positive energy out of the room. They are more than happy to make us feel miserable so that they can feel better. All take, no give. You don't need to own their problems.

There's a simple solution: break the relationship.

I've done it a couple of times, and it felt terrible because the toxic person was a friend. It's not easy at first, but the payoff is worth it. It's harder to do with family, but, for the most part, you may be able to limit the time spent with an energy-sucking relative.

Toxic Environment: A toxic environment may be more difficult to shake. When I worked in the jail, everything about the place was poisonous. I made the decision to leave the sheriff's office and went back to working as a street cop in a city. There were still many toxic situations, but at least I was able to get away from the negativity now and then.

One result of working too long in a toxic environment is that some of us end up using unhealthy coping mechanisms for dealing with unhappiness and stress. Excessive drinking and drug use are the main offenders, but gambling, sex addiction, and even self-isolation are horrible ways to cope.

My advice for anyone struggling with addiction is to build positive relationships and dump the toxic folks and situations. Even if it means changing locales and careers, make happiness the priority instead of status or financial success.

CHAPTER
EIGHT
BE WELL

Therapy Session

My legs felt like stumps of wet clay as I shuffled to my chair in Ursula's office. I flopped onto the seat cushion, leaden arms resting on my lap, and stared at the floor.

"Uh-oh," Ursula uttered as she took her seat. "What's wrong, Scott?"

I hunched over and wrapped my arms around my knees. I looked up and tried to muster a smile, but I knew my eyes had that dullness, evident in the chronically depressed.

"Remember the class I signed up for to become a peer support volunteer?" I asked.

"I do. It was so you could help other addicts. The class started last week, right?"

I sat up, slid my damp hands across my jeans, and

tried to melt back into the big chair. "I had a full-blown panic attack the first day of class and had to leave," I confessed, "So basically, I'm a worthless piece of shit." Hearing it out loud dragged me even further down into the abyss.

"Said the man who's saved many lives," Ursula pointed out.

I closed my eyes, and we sat in silence for a moment. I'd been ready to slip into a serious bout of depression, but her comment short-circuited my resolve.

"You're just not ready yet for something as intense as peer counseling," she clarified with one of her room-brightening smiles. "It's all about self-care, Scott. You know that. You can't help other people unless you first take care of yourself."

I opened my eyes. "What if I'm never ready?"

Ursula shrugged. "Then, you'll do something else to help people."

An odd sense of relief spread through my body like a long drink of cool water on a hot summer day. I looked out the big window and took two slow, easy breaths. I really wanted that training, not only to help other addicts, but also to feel better about myself. To gain some shred of self-worth back in my life, but maybe I wasn't quite ready to take on others' pain.

I felt better. It wasn't that long ago that the despair I felt over leaving the class would've taken days to get over. I smiled.

"There it is." Ursula nodded her approval. "What brought that smile on?"

"I was thinking about how I fully expected to be slammed by a wave of shame when I walked out of that classroom."

"It wasn't like that?" she asked.

"Not at all. It hit me that my classmates were all addicts and that they only felt sympathy for me. There was no judgment."

"They've all been there," she agreed. "Well, you look more relaxed now. Shall we dig into some more of your history?"

I gave my hands one final brush on my jeans and squared my shoulders. "Dig away."

"Last time we talked, you mentioned that you quit the sheriff's office and went to work for the city police department," she recapped. "Did you suffer any more injuries during that part of your career?"

"Plenty," I said. "I've had a total of 13 surgeries over the years. A blown disk in my lower back. Torn cartilage in both knees. Torn rotator cuff, and, yes, lots of pain relievers were prescribed each time."

"Did you ever think you were becoming addicted to opioids?"

"Not at that point," I replied. "In fact, I didn't figure that out until many years later. I do remember the pills starting not to work as well as they had in the past. And, I recall getting easily irritated when I stopped taking them. I just didn't put two and two together back then."

"You were already building tolerance and suffering from minor withdrawals," she translated.

"And, I was pushing myself even harder to succeed."

"In what way?"

"I got my master's degree during that time and started teaching academic classes at police academies and colleges," I explained. "I was also trained as an instructor in hand-to-hand techniques and impact weapons. I joined the SWAT team and was promoted to sergeant."

"That's a lot of hats," Ursula commented.

"I remember one day wearing my regular uniform to work my shift, changing into SWAT gear for training, changing into gym clothes to teach a baton class, and then donning a suit and tie to teach a college class that night."

She gave me a knowing smile. "Still trying to please your dad, I see."

I rubbed my hand over my face. "Yup. I guess."

"Tell me about the new job at the city PD," Ursula said. "The one after you wisely decided to stop working in the jail."

"I wish I could say I mellowed out and took fewer risks, but that wasn't the case."

———

The old clapboard cottage was completely engulfed in flames.

I got on the radio, gave an update, and pulled into a gravel parking lot near the house. A small, wide-eyed crowd had already gathered. I got out of my patrol car and was relieved to see no one had strayed too close to the danger zone. I was approached by an elderly gentleman, wringing his hands. "Officer," he said. "There's still someone inside."

I glanced at the cottage. The roiling columns of flame had climbed ten feet higher than when I arrived only moments earlier. *Anyone inside is already dead*, I thought to myself.

"Are you positive?" I asked.

"Yes, sir," he answered. "There's an older lady who lives there alone. She has a little dog. Her name is Cate. The lady, not the dog. I walked up there before the fire got too big and saw her standin' in the middle of the hallway, not movin', just standin' there!"

"Was she trapped from getting out?"

"Maybe," he said frantically. "But, I don't think so. You see, she's a little off. She gets easily confused."

"Thanks," I said. "I'll check it out. Make sure to keep your distance."

"No problem there." He scampered back to the growing crowd of spectators.

It's amazing how fast fire can move, especially when someone like me opens the door and feeds in more oxygen. I called for help on my radio and ran up to the house. The flames were already climbing well above the roofline. A few windows had already blown out, so maybe the backdraft wouldn't be too bad. I tried to peer into the windows, but there was too much smoke. Knowing the doorknob was likely as hot as the sun, I kicked the door in.

No backdraft, thank God.

I headed into the living room. "Cate, are you in here?" I called out. No response. Flames crawled up the walls like snakes, and thick, black smoke rippled like water along the ceiling.

If I kept low, the visibility wasn't too bad. It wasn't a very big house, and a quick glance into the kitchen confirmed no one was in there. I began to cough and was soon drenched in sweat. My lungs screamed at me to back off and get the hell out of there. I plunged ahead through a short hallway and into what seemed to be the only bedroom.

It wasn't at all what I expected. The whole room was on fire, the flames licking the bed. And there was Cate, lying on that bed completely naked, smoking a cigarette like she didn't have a care in the world. Her chihuahua was at the foot of the bed, shaking like a leaf.

She was very scrawny, and I quickly scooped her up and ran back out the way I'd entered. The dog had the good sense to follow.

Another police car and a fire rig pulled up as I jogged away with her. Cate was still smoking the cigarette.

I sat her in the passenger seat of my patrol car and covered her with a yellow emergency blanket. Fortunately, it wasn't long until an ambulance pulled up. The paramedics rushed in, and I told them what happened, which only resulted in raised eyebrows.

Those guys see it all.

Therapy Session cont.

"What a wild story," Ursula remarked.

"Like they say, truth is stranger than fiction."

"It is indeed," she replied. "You mentioned that you felt obligated to go into that burning cottage. Do you think that's what every officer would do?"

"Not necessarily. No one would blame anyone else for not going in properly equipped. I actually got a Medal of Valor for that little encounter. But if I had been injured in there, someone else could've been put at risk trying to save me. I would've added to the problem. I guess there's a fine line between courage and stupidity."

"Or poor judgment," Ursula clarified. "But, you do have a pattern of taking risks. I'm not sure it's such a good idea to give out medals if it encourages such risks. I mean, I'm not judging your actions. You saved that woman's life."

"Taking risks," I said, smiling again. "You pretty much summed up my entire career."

"Two smiles in one day," Ursula commented. "I think we're onto something."

Survival Tips

Every time you fly on a commercial airliner, you're reminded—in case of an emergency—to put on your oxygen mask before putting one on your child. The reason? You need to be able to breathe before you can help your toddler.

It took me decades to understand that I personally needed to become well in order to finally do any good for others. I needed to get healthy before I could help other addicts.

Nothing new here that we haven't all heard a thousand times, but it works. That's why we've heard it a thousand times. The main point is to take care of yourself first, before reaching out to others.

Get Out in Nature: I was fortunate that during some of the darkest days of my addiction and recovery, I was able to spend an enormous amount of time in nature. My wife and I served as campground hosts at a number of national and state parks from the Sierra Nevada and Rocky Mountains to the Florida Keys. Even hanging out in a neighborhood park is fine. Just get outside and get some sunshine on your face. Can't get outside? Research shows that watching videos of nature helps, too.

Make Connections: My wife and I once lived in a community with the following clubs, or guilds, as they call them: Bridge Guild, Concert Guild, Dinner Guild (foodies), Folk Guild (dancing), Games Guild, Gardeners Guild, Library Guild, Writers Guild, Scholars Guild, Shakespeare Guild, and the Swim

Guild. That's a lot of opportunities to connect. Try finding a community of shared interests near you and join up. If you don't like certain ones that you've tried, try something else until you find a good fit and feel comfortable.

Exercise and Diet: There are times when I can't lift anything with my left arm or even walk. I face those challenges to this day. But I can still sit in a chair and do some qigong. I can still get in the water and move around.

As far as diet, I'm not going to rant on about eating your vegetables and whole grains because you already know that. I will add that a brain damaged by drugs does need a certain amount of protein, so if you have a vegan or vegetarian diet, do the research and make sure that you're getting enough.

The above habits and practices can often be easily combined. I can take a walk with some friends while eating broccoli and cover all the bases.

When I started to feel better physically and emotionally, I was able to commit some of my newfound energy toward helping others. Although I'd like to claim solely altruistic reasons, I have to admit that I also got a spiritual and emotional boost from helping someone in need.

Having a sense of worth and purpose are crucial to recovery. What better way to build your shattered self-esteem than by helping others? We'll talk more about that later. Before plunging in and sprinting down the road of doing good, I recommend trying at least one thing that is solely your own. Start by getting yourself healthy.

Therapy Session

I looked out the rippled window of my therapist's office. The leaves on the cottonwood trees were turning gold. Autumn was here, and Ursula was clad in a sage green cashmere sweater that looked soft enough to float on.

"Last session, you said you spent eight years with the city PD," she began. "What happened after that?"

"I changed careers and taught college full-time," I replied. "I had my master's degree and spent a few years teaching college part-time, and decided to give full-time a go."

"What brought on such a huge change?"

"It was a mistake, actually. My wife and I were starting a family, and it occurred to me that police work might not be the best thing for a guy who was planning to be part of his kids' lives. It wasn't just dangerous; the shift work was rough. I remember when I was first promoted to sergeant and had to work what was called the relief shift. It was two graveyards, followed by two swings, followed by one day shift. I felt like a zombie."

"Really unhealthy," Ursula commented. "But, you said teaching college was a mistake. Why is that?"

"Teaching full-time just didn't work for me. There were two main reasons that being a cop was a good fit for me: first, it felt great to help people, and second, I loved the rush."

"Back to being an adrenaline junkie."

"Yeah, I guess so. I returned to police work and started at the bottom. I got a job at the Grants Pass Department of Public Safety in Oregon, where I was both a police officer and a firefighter."

"How did that work out?" she asked.

"Pretty well, although I wasn't a big fan of the firefighting part. Too physical. I got right back into the swing of things and became a SWAT team leader. Because of my experience, I was quickly promoted to lieutenant, in charge of operations."

"Did you stay with that agency long?" Ursula asked.

"Just a couple of years," I replied. "A police chief position opened up in the nearby city of Ashland, and I went for it. It was a college town with lots of tourist dollars pouring in. But, it was still small enough that I could get out of the office now and then and do some police work."

"Being Chief of Police wasn't police work?" Her brows rose.

"I suppose it was. But most of the time, I did things to ensure the rest of the department had what they needed to do their jobs. Budget, rules and regulations, policies, and so on."

"So, you missed the rush?"

I nodded. "I did, but, like I said, it was a small enough agency that I could still get into the middle of some hands-on involvement now and then."

————

A young man pointed a gun at two teenage girls. Then, he put the business end of the big revolver against his temple. The three of them were sitting at a small café table inside Cantwell's grocery store. The kind of table that shoppers use after buying a Starbucks and a cup of soup. No one else was in the store—it'd already been evacuated, and uniformed patrol officers were covering the various exits.

A stand-off.

"What do you think, Chief?" asked Kris, the on-duty sergeant. "Should we call SWAT?"

I watched through a window as the young man once again pointed the handgun at each girl and then returned it to his head.

"I don't think they'd get here in time, Sarge."

Minutes earlier, I'd been bored out of my mind at a weekly city council meeting. As the police chief, my attendance was mandatory, even though I was rarely called upon by the mayor or other council members. Most of the city's business concerned building permits, public works projects, and other non-police-related topics. That was fine by me.

Then, my portable radio came to life with the call of a man with a gun. In a small town, that meant *everyone* responded.

"I think he's serious," Kris said. "We could rush him."

"We could," I agreed, "but the first uniform he sees might push him into shooting those girls."

"Any recommendations?"

I knew the gun-wielding young man meant business. We just didn't have time to place a sniper or call a tactical team. Then, something occurred to me. I looked down at my clothes.

"I'm going in," I said.

"That's nuts," Kris blurted. "No disrespect, Chief."

"Do you have any other ideas?"

"Fresh out."

"I'm the only one not in a uniform," I said. "I'll just walk in through the front door like a customer and do whatever has to be done."

"You're crazy, but you're the boss."

I headed for the sliding glass door at the store's entrance and walked in. My handgun was within easy reach and covered by my sports coat. The table where the trio sat was only about fifty feet away, and the guy's back was to me. If either of the girls saw me, they didn't react.

So far, so good.

My plan was to announce myself and demand that he put down his gun. I got within range, slowly lowered my hand to my holster, and drew my gun.

Then, he pulled the trigger.

The sound was deafening. Everything turned to molasses. I watched the young man's head jerk sideways. The bullet punched a hole through his right temple and exited via a much larger hole on the left side of his skull. Both girls screamed, jumped up, and sprinted past me.

I holstered my gun. His heart continued to beat for a couple of seconds, pumping squirts of blood against the concrete wall. His body slumped to the ground.

Therapy Session cont.

Ursula didn't say anything for a moment. Just nodded her head. Then, she cleared her throat.

"And, you wonder why you have so much stored trauma," she finally said. "What happened after that?"

"I just went back to the city council meeting and tried to forget about it."

"Your body doesn't forget that kind of trauma." Ursula tugged down the sleeves of her sweater as if my story had sent an icy chill through her. "Even though it's the nature of the job, it seems like you're drawn to reckless behavior like a moth to a flame."

"I'm beginning to realize that," I agreed. "Even after my career was over, I still got involved in some dicey situations. Some I could've avoided, some I couldn't, but I'm doing better about that these days. I've finally decided that it's okay to let the younger folks take care of the heroics."

"Glad to hear it," Ursula approved. "Did you have any more surgeries or injuries while you were police chief?"

"Several. Mostly my back and neck. More drugs were prescribed before, during, and after. I was in constant pain."

"How about drinks?"

I smiled. "No, thanks. I quit years ago."

Ursula laughed. "Very funny. I'm glad you've maintained a sense of humor."

"Yes, I was still drinking too much back then," I admitted. "I worked way too many hours each day, and the stress was intense. Especially the politics and personnel issues."

Ursula raised an eyebrow. "More intense than all that violence and bloodshed?"

"In many ways. The single hardest thing I ever faced in my career was having to fire my close friend, Julie. I terminated her for grabbing and twisting the arm of another employee. In fact, exactly one year after that termination, I completely fell apart physically and mentally. That was the beginning of the end for my law enforcement career."

"Why did you have to fire Julie?"

"She was a captain and second-in-command after me. We'd had a call of a crazy skinhead threatening people with a rifle on the Fourth of July. Julie had been up for hours afterward, working on a press release. She was reading aloud the release and mispronounced the word yarmulke. One of our dispatchers was standing near her and corrected Julie on how to say it. Julie stood up, grabbed the dispatcher, and twisted her arm. I terminated her. She sued. It got really ugly."

"What you did doesn't sound unreasonable," Ursula commented. "Besides Julie being your friend, why do you think it had such a negative impact on you to fire her?"

I felt a stab of pain in my gut and took a deep breath.

"I often felt like we betrayed each other," I confessed. "I know I did my job. I did things right, but I also had the feeling that I didn't do the right thing. Like, I had gone against my personal code of conduct."

"Do you mean like the Code of Silence?" Ursula asked. "Police need to protect each other?"

I flexed my hands a few times, surprised that my breathing was even. Thinking about firing my friend usually spun me out.

"Not really," I replied. "It was more like my responsibility to take care of my people. I really cared about Julie. The termination was such a final act. It ended her entire career. There was little chance she could ever get another job in law enforcement."

"Unfortunately, that was the nature of your position. It was your responsibility. I think you need to let it go and practice a little self-forgiveness."

"Maybe."

Survival Tips

I was passionate about my career. Being the knight in shining armor who slays the dragon and saves the day isn't too far from how I saw myself. It feels great to help someone in need. But, I over-identified with my chosen path, which brings up the age-old question: Who am I?

Many people are intensely committed to their careers. Teachers are a great example of people who are more interested in expanding minds than making money. The vast majority of cops I knew entered law enforcement with a strong desire to help people who were in crisis. They certainly weren't in for the kudos, money, or great working hours.

I saw myself as a cop, through and through. But when I lost my career, what was I? Certainly, I was a father and a husband. Since both of my parents were dead, was I still even a son?

These survival tips are about letting go of the past. There is nothing wrong with being successful. Accomplishments support self-worth and self-esteem.

Accomplishments also feed the ego, which can lead to warped perceptions. When I lost my health, I was forced to take a hard look at my priorities. I could no longer physically or mentally be the warrior riding to the defense of the innocent. I could no longer be the man who led the charge.

Past Labels: Make a list of all the labels that you've accumulated over the years from childhood to present (son, college student, wife, teacher, cop, nurse, tennis player, lawyer, marathon runner, sister, drug addict, etc.).

Current Labels: Make a list of all your current labels (husband, grandmother, cook, artist, gardener, brother, recovering addict, etc.).

Which labels have gone away? Which ones have stayed? Which labels are new?

How did it feel to have some of those titles stripped away? What's left? The lesson I learned was that none of these labels, even my current ones, are really who I am. Things change. Identities change. Maybe it's time to let some of those labels go.

When I was at my lowest point and had checked myself into residential treatment for suicidal ideation, I met with a psychiatrist who lit a spark in the back of my mind. He told me it was time to put down the sword. He said my days serving as a warrior were done.

I would've been pretty bummed out if he'd stopped right there, but he went on to ask what I thought about becoming a wounded healer. That's a label I'd be proud to wear.

CHAPTER
TEN
OPIOID WITHDRAWALS

Therapy Session

I was in pain. I guess it showed. I eased into the overstuffed chair and winced. I'd been tortured for years with severe nerve pain that started in my lower back and traveled down my left sciatica—a product of too many injuries and too many unnecessary surgeries.

"You're hurting, aren't you?" asked my ever-observant therapist. Today, Ursula was dressed in a rust-colored short-sleeve top and a pair of sky-blue pants that matched her desert-themed artwork. I wondered if it was intentional.

"Bad week," I said. "All those years fighting opioid addiction sometimes overshadows why I started taking that crap in the first place."

"I've been thinking about that since our last talk.

How all those opioids you took over the years became less and less effective at controlling the pain."

I tried to shift in the chair to ease the agony, but to no avail.

"Have you ever heard of the term hyperalgesia?" she asked. "Or Opioid-Induced Hyperalgesia?"

"I have," I replied. "Feeling more pain after being on opioids too long."

"More and more studies have shown that opioids are a poor choice for long-term pain relief," she explained. "They're great for acute pain, like right after surgery, but a bad idea for someone like you."

Someone like me. I'd heard that before. My anger was now at a full boil. I clenched my fists until they turned white.

"Then, why did the fucking doctors keep prescribing stronger ones if they knew that?"

"A very valid point." She sat back in her chair. "I think part of it was they just didn't know enough about it back when you were being treated. It's getting better, but the opioid crisis is still a huge public health problem."

I unclenched my fists and rubbed my palms on my jeans. "I'll tell you what I think," I said. "The pharmaceutical companies are making a shitload of money off other people's suffering. It's criminal. And some of the doctors are buying into it."

"Do you want to take a break? Maybe walk around a little?" Ursula suggested.

I hopped out of my chair and strode to the big

window. "I realize I'm the one who abused the drugs, and I do take responsibility for that," I said. "But all of that arrogance and ignorance from the doctors makes me mad. How could they not know how addictive this stuff is?"

"They're learning."

"I'd like to just get one good punch in on one of those guys," I said, spinning around. "Or better yet, shoot them full of opioids until they're addicted and let them experience the living hell of withdrawal."

"I get it," Ursula replied, her tone neutral.

I recognized that my anger was getting the best of me. I dropped my shoulders, walked back to my chair, and flopped down. Tears welled in my eyes. I reached for the cardboard tissue box, but instead of pulling one out, I crushed the box in my hand and dropped it in my lap.

To Ursula's credit, she let me have my tantrum. We sat in silence for a while, and, after a more appropriate use of the demolished tissues, I calmed down.

"Are you okay with talking about what happened after your career?" she asked, abruptly changing the subject.

"It was a horror show," I said, sitting up straight. "First of all, there was all the guilt and shame about losing my job and income. I wasn't there for my wife and kids. I felt that I was flawed somehow. Weak and worthless."

"Do you feel that way now?"

"No," I said. "But, it took over fifteen years to reach that point."

"During that time, were you still in chronic pain and taking opioids?"

"I was."

"I know you made a few attempts to get off opioids. Tell me about the first time."

———

For an hour of non-stop screaming, this particular bathroom was ideal. The old split-level house had three bathrooms. Two had windows. This one did not. It was in the dead center of our hillside home, on a large lot, hemmed in on three sides by old-growth incense cedars and towering ponderosa pines. It was the most logical room in the place to contain the noise.

Or at least, to keep the neighbors from calling the police.

Determined as I was to stop taking the prescription opioids, I let out another primal scream. This one started as a low moan, paying tribute to the relentless pain in my back, knees, and shoulders. Like a wounded tiger trapped in a cage, I was ready to lash out at anything.

I was glad I'd waited until my wife was at work and our sons were at school. My body shivered so hard that even the brown sleeping bag draped over my shoulders did little to keep the chills at bay. It was

74 degrees in the house, but I swore I was freezing to death.

This was my first major opioid withdrawal.

I tried to concentrate on why I had decided to stop using my pain meds. It may have been that I'd run out early, which was becoming a disturbing pattern, but part of it was the horrible side effects.

My sex drive had crashed and burned. Constipation was so complete that no home enema kit stood a chance. Clarity of thought was a thing of the past.

I slumped to the cool, pink tile on the bathroom floor. My limbs hummed with needle-like pain, like when your arm wakes up after having been slept on for too long. An ice-cold burn that reached deep into my tissue. Hordes of frozen ants swarmed my entire body.

Exhausted by my own screaming, I broke into an oily sweat. Rank, toxic perspiration seeped from my pores and drenched my 49ers t-shirt and dark gray sweatpants. I shed the sleeping bag, stripped off my soaked clothing, and threw them in the tub. I reached up, yanked on a towel, and sent the bar crashing to the floor.

As I wrapped the towel around my shoulders, more chills set in to oppose the recent bout of sweats. Thousands of needles pricked my skin, and I couldn't stop shaking. The fetid sweat was still there, turning frigid as it cooled off my body way too quickly.

The depression was almost as bad as the

withdrawals. It was like being in deep, dark water. A blanket of lead enveloped my body and wore me down. Other times, I felt rage at the bad hand I'd been dealt.

Or, was it the hand I had chosen?

Suicidal thoughts—such as renting a car, driving it into a storage unit, and leaving the engine running—crept into my brain.

I knew I couldn't turn to my doctors for help; I didn't want any more medications. Their drug of choice was usually a selective serotonin reuptake inhibitor (SSRI). Then, I would experience the joys of erectile dysfunction, my skull buzzing so badly that I couldn't move my head without getting dizzy, and let's not forget the weight gain.

Bottom line: the drugs did absolutely nothing to stop my depression.

I broke away from my despair and looked around the bathroom. I couldn't let my kids see me like this. It was time to clean up the mess and get dressed.

Therapy Session cont.

"So, you finally figured out that most of your pain and depression were connected to the opioids," Ursula commented.

"Yes." It was odd how drained I felt after talking about the withdrawals. Drained, but much more at ease now that the rage was ebbing away. "I realized that by continually going to my docs, I was just getting myself in deeper. Remember OxyContin?"

"I do," she replied.

"Hillbilly Heroin is what we called it in recovery," I said. "All you had to do was chew the time-release tablet, and it would send the opioids shooting into your brain. That's how I was doing it, leading up to the bathroom screaming sessions. They prescribed it to me like candy on Halloween."

"Opioids are often overprescribed," Ursula commented, "but more knowledge is out there now, and it's getting better. As are you."

Survival Tips

Addiction and mental illness go hand in hand. In my case, Major Depressive Disorder (MDD) and anxiety were the culprits. Even if the potential for major depression was there before I got hooked on opioids, it wasn't until I tried to get off of them that I experienced the above afflictions.

Opioids are prescribed for the short-term relief of acute pain, but they suck for chronic pain relief. For me, it reached the point where the constant use of opioids hijacked my body's natural ability to produce all those feel-good brain chemicals, such as serotonin and dopamine.

The prolonged use of opioids made me feel *more* pain. And, it wasn't just from building a tolerance to the drug. Once the flow of opioids stopped, my brain didn't have any ability to produce those chemicals.

Unfortunately, recovery is a road without end. During my first attempt to get off opioids, it took two and a half years before opioid withdrawals stopped wracking my body. Thirty months of writhing throughout the night while my flesh crawled with what I call "ice-ants".

DO NOT TAKE OPIOIDS FOR LONG-TERM PAIN RELIEF. Just don't do it.

I strongly recommend that you get a second opinion before taking any medication that will hijack the body's natural resources for coping.

When I was in rehab, one of the first questions asked by my fellow addicts was, "What are you in for?" They were asking what my drug, or drugs, of choice were. Although many of the clients were also hooked on alcohol and street drugs, I was surprised to see how many were in rehab for misusing prescription drugs. The most popular prescription drugs were opioids (such as hydrocodone and fentanyl), benzos or other anti-anxiety drugs, amphetamines (such as Adderall), and sleeping meds and tranquilizers (such as Ambien and Valium)

All of these meds are highly addictive and should be reserved for situations such as surgery or a mental health crisis. I strongly believe they are horrible choices for long-term health outcomes.

It is our underlying trauma that leads to addiction and mental illness. Until that trauma is processed, no amount of pharmaceuticals will provide long-term healing.

CHAPTER
ELEVEN
DETOX

Therapy Session

"Last session, you talked about your first major withdrawal," Ursula began. "You suffered through it, but it finally ended. And then you moved to Maui. What brought that on?"

"My wife and I had been to the islands a few times and loved them," I answered as I stared at the floor. "I was in constant pain, so the warm weather was helpful. Swimming in the saltwater was a good way to get some exercise when I couldn't do much walking."

"You went through another round of opioid withdrawals in Hawaii?"

I lifted my eyes. Ursula was once again wearing a sweater. This one was a knit, sky-blue number sporting white snowflakes sprinkled across the shoulders and neckline. A festive nod to the coming holidays. "I did."

"That means, obviously, that you slipped back into using opioids at some point after the first time you kicked it."

She was right. I'd been through so much suffering that I could no longer even track the timeline. I put my elbows on my knees and covered my face with both hands.

"What happened, Scott?" she asked. I could sense that she moved a little closer, but she was careful not to make contact.

"I just simply switched my drug of choice." I dropped my hands into my lap and sat up. "Although I didn't know that back then."

"Go on."

"When we first moved to Hawaii, I was still drinking alcohol. I had my first and only blackout episode from drinking way too much scotch. I've never had a drink again after that. Then, the pain started to get much worse, and I did something I never would've dreamed possible after my first round of withdrawals."

"You went back on pain meds."

I grimaced. "In a big way. Morphine, Oxycodone. All prescribed, of course. It didn't take long to start abusing."

"Unfortunately, the addictive mind is very clever," Ursula replied. "You used alcohol as a coping mechanism for constant pain and depression. Once that stopped, you no longer had a way to escape and numb yourself. How long did you stay on those drugs?"

"I really can't remember." My heart started hammering in my chest. Although I was beginning to feel safe around my counselor, I could sense shame starting to worm its way into my brain.

Ursula leaned forward once again. "We don't have to talk about this, okay?"

I took a deep breath and reached for my trusty anti-anxiety bracelets. "No. It's fine. I truly can't recall how long I was on those meds," I said. "About a year, I think. All I remember was three trips to the psych ward for suicidal ideation. On the third trip, they got sick of me, and I was shipped off to the county-run detox center for my second, and far worse, round of withdrawals."

"Tell me about it."

———

"Wallet, keys, money, phone, and anything else in your pockets goes right here," the young woman instructed in a pleasantly bored tone.

I was at the front desk of the Mahalo House, which was an upbeat name for the detox center on Maui. Knowing I would have little need of my wallet or keys, I'd already left them with my tearful wife just moments before. I reluctantly gave up my phone, losing the last means of connection with the outside world. They replaced my phone with a threadbare wool blanket, a scratchy bath towel no bigger than a hand towel, and some sheets that I later learned were far too small for my bed.

A man with massive shoulders and long black hair escorted me from the registration desk through the lush, overgrown grounds and past a couple of buildings. His name was Kim. Not a common name for a man, but this guy was way too big to bring that up.

"Don't talk to anyone from those housing units," were the first words spoken by my guide as he pointed vaguely to his right. "You're in the detox barracks and can have no interaction with the guys in the recovery program."

I said nothing. This was my first experience with recovery centers, so I had no idea what he meant. I was drifting in and out of the first wave of withdrawal symptoms, and even the tropical breeze gave me chills so deep that I couldn't keep my body from shivering. It was all I could do to focus on the path that led past a dilapidated dining hall the size of a high school gym.

What was happening to me? I was a middle-class white guy working my way toward sixty who'd enjoyed a highly successful career, raised two sons, and was still deeply in love with my wife. I had no place being in a county-run rehab center, but I was living on an island where my insurance didn't cover getting off prescription opioids.

I nodded to the broad-backed gentleman in a

lame attempt to let him know I understood the rules about mixing with the other prisoners, but it didn't matter since he was walking ahead of me. He was probably used to leading an assortment of chemically altered zombies to their bunks and just rambled on without waiting to see if anything sank in.

We approached a sagging porch with an overhang that was somehow defying gravity. It was so rotten, I imagined termites holding the whole thing up. A small-screen TV rested on a half-inch laminate shelf that sagged just like the porch.

To my left, sitting in a chair that only a chiropractor could love, slouched a man in his late thirties. His beard was at the point that could either be considered careless or rough-and-tumble. He looked to be both, but still jumped up, turned the volume down on the miniature TV with what seemed like a plastic fork embedded into the bottom of the set, and extended his hand.

"Dan. I'm in for benzos," said my fellow inmate.

I shook his hand. "Glad to meet you." It was an automatic response. I wasn't glad to meet him or anyone else in this fetid compound. It struck me that I couldn't just walk away from this place. For one thing, I was in the middle of a mountainside jungle, miles away from any town. And, I had signed my freedom away when I "volunteered" to be committed to the detox center, where I would ride out the opioid withdrawals for a week or so.

Kim cleared his throat. He obviously had other

detox patients waiting for the tour. "See that barracks over there?"

I looked at a building almost identical to ours a few yards away, half-hidden in the dense, green overgrowth of hibiscus, birds of paradise, bougainvillea, and plumeria.

"I see it," I answered.

"Stay away from that building, too. In fact, you can only be in and around the detox barracks, unless it's time for chow. I'll show you your room. It's almost time for dinner, but there's no bell or anything. You need to be on time."

Not only did I not have a watch, but I also didn't have my cell phone to tell me what time it was. Maybe there was a clock in my room.

Kim yanked on the door. It was stuck. He put his considerable bulk into it, and it finally gave way.

"The door sticks," my big guide drawled.

Besides the shakes that were wracking my body, every one of my joints ached. I'd had this wild delusion over the past few months that a detox center would be all white sheets, puffy pillows, gentle nurses who called me "hon," and fresh fruit smoothies. I was still shocked that this facility was all my medical insurance would provide.

We walked down the hall. There were four rooms with two bunks in each. Mine was second on the right. First thing I saw: a giant cockroach—the kind that only gets that big in the tropics—hiss and scurry across the scarred wooden floor where it hid under a pile of clothes next to the bunk on my right. So, I chose the bunk on my left.

The second thing that hit me was the smell of mildew that clung to every surface.

Third, there was no clock.

"I gotta head back to intake, Brah," Kim said. "Good luck."

The look in my guide's eyes was sincere enough. It was a mixture of pity, feigned cheerfulness, and apathy that was likely the best he could manage after dealing with folks like me all day.

I put the bedding on the bunk and set my single duffle on the floor. There was no dresser, closet, or bed stand. Not even a few nails in the wall to hold my belongings. The duffle would have to do. Or I could just set everything in a pile at the foot of the bunk. Hoping that the duffle would keep out the cockroaches, centipedes, and rats, I zipped it closed.

The thin mattress was stuffed into a rubberized cover meant to keep all the puke, diarrhea, urine, and other bodily fluids from soaking in. I tried to put my issued sheets on the slick mattress. They were too short.

It was almost dinner time. I only knew this because people were starting to migrate toward the dining hall. I had yet to see a clock, so I followed the crowd. It began to rain as I walked the open pathway. It was a warm, humid rain, unique to the climate, but its cooling effect woke up my ice-ants, which led to uncontrollable shaking.

Cautious not to talk to anyone outside the detox

dorm, I shuffled through the line and got a generous portion of white rice and beef drowned in rich brown gravy. Always mindful of a balanced diet, I gave the nod to the young woman wielding a giant spoon and got a scoop of steamed vegetables.

The beverages were limited to coffee, which I hate, and two colors of opaque liquids in uncomplimentary, clear, plastic dispensers that must've held ten gallons each. One was pale red. The other was a pale yellow. I went for the yellow, which made the gravy on my beef look a shade grayer.

The cafeteria line was a mixed group of men and women, aged from their early thirties to their late seventies. Mostly a jumble of locals clad in t-shirts, board shorts, and flip-flops. I fit right in with my island tan, shorts, and the only tank top I owned that didn't have a microbrewery logo emblazoned on the chest. Any clothing displaying drugs, alcohol, and even certain rock-and-roll bands was prohibited and confiscated upon our arrival.

Fewer clothes to soak up the night sweats.

I sat down, nodded to a couple of guys I hoped were from the detox dorm, and dug in. I immediately became nauseated but managed to swallow the food. It wasn't the taste, which was actually quite wholesome: typical island fare, even without the Spam, but the dope sickness was coming on strong, and I simply couldn't stomach any food. I made it to my room in time to collapse on the narrow cot at about the same time the sun was setting.

It turned out that I shared the room with Darth

Vader—the poor guy was detoxing off a wine habit of five bottles per day and had severe sleep apnea. He had one of those continuous positive airway pressure machines, or what he called his CPAP, that kept his airway open all night.

Purely from exhaustion, I fell asleep for almost two hours. I woke up freezing, completely drenched in sweat. I got up, changed clothes, and tried to crawl back into bed, but the sheets were still soaked. I put the thin towel under my shoulders and a t-shirt over my drenched pillow. I fell asleep for a short while, but Darth's breathing machine woke me up. In truth, I kept hoping for a red lightsaber to flash on in the middle of the night. At that point in my detox from OxyContin, morphine, and Oxycodone, a quick death by Vader would've been most welcome.

I was still sweating, so I rolled out of bed, out the door, and down a dimly lit hallway that ended at a nurses' station. I woke up the nurse.

"I can't stand it. I'm freezing, my joints are killing me, and it feels like bugs are crawling all over me," I said. "Isn't there anything you can do?"

"Not much," she answered as she searched my file. "How about some antihistamine? That might help with the itching and might make you drowsy."

I knew it wouldn't do either. For some reason, antihistamines perk me up like a visit to Starbucks.

"How about a shower?" I pleaded. In past withdrawals, I remembered the warm shower helping a bit with the ice-ants.

"Sorry," she answered. "That's not possible in the

middle of the night. Maybe in a few hours. We wouldn't want to wake up the other patients now, would we?"

I frankly didn't give a shit about the other patients, but kept it to myself. I staggered back to my room and fell to my knees. I crawled to my soaked bed, but it was miserable. I stripped off all my wet clothes and the drenched sheets. I pulled out my final long-sleeve t-shirt and my one pair of sweatpants and shrugged on the fresh, dry clothes. I laid the old duffel bag under me to absorb some of the moisture and climbed into bed. The single blanket was too wet, so it remained on the floor, along with the spongy, Chiclet-sized pillow.

In only two hours, I managed to sweat through the new layers.

I stumbled out of bed, into the hallway, and out the exit door. A sliver of sun bathed a patch of gravel near the exit. I saw a beach chair with only one of the seat straps intact leaning against the dorm wall. I grabbed the chair, moved to the spot where the sunlight was creeping in, and felt slightly warmed. I sat there until I noticed a few people zombie-shuffling to the cafeteria. I followed and was rewarded with some hot tea. I still couldn't stomach any food.

And so, my days and nights continued for a week. I'd become fast friends with Benzo Dan, and we enjoyed such movies as *What About Bob?* and *28 Days.*

So long as we didn't lose the plastic fork to work the volume.

On the morning of my seventh day, I met a guy at

breakfast named Franco. He had been in the recovery program for over a month. Young guy. Talkative. A thief by his own admission. He was the cause of the yogurt crisis that started a couple of days after my arrival. He had taken more than his fair share of Yoplait Yogurt from a cooler that patients were supposed to keep out of. He finally got caught. The entire compound was denied yogurt for two days.

A couple of hours after meeting Franco, I hung out on the detox porch with Benzo Dan. He was watching *CaddyShack*, and I was too sick to do anything but stare off into space as I slowly slid off the hard plastic chair.

Franco walked up and offered me some opioids.

It was a pivotal moment for me. I could've taken them, and my suffering would end. Well, temporarily. In an exceptional moment of courage, I thanked the young man but turned down the meds.

Not that it mattered in the long run.

Therapy Session cont.

Ursula steepled her fingers and sat back in her chair. "What did you mean when you said that turning down those opioids didn't matter in the long run?" she asked. "You said that it was an exceptional moment of courage."

I'd thought my shame attack had faded, but it reared up again.

"Those were dark times," I said. "I left Mahalo House after eight days, not because I was over my withdrawals, but because I was not getting any better. It wasn't the best place for going through such intense symptoms. I'll never forget the sense of relief I got when my wife pulled up and drove me home. Most of the relief was just being with her."

"I like how you focused on how good it was to be with your wife," Ursula said. "How long did that second episode of withdrawals last?"

"Three weeks. That's how long until I couldn't stand the skin-crawling. My whole nervous system was waking up, and I was on fire. I remember I couldn't even trim my fingernails because the sensation was too painful."

I folded my arms across my chest and grabbed each shoulder.

Ursula stood up. "I've got an idea," she said. "Are you up for taking a walk?"

I released my shoulders but kept my arms crossed. "Uh, sure. What do you have in mind?"

"There's a holiday market going on this week just a block up the street. Let's stroll up there along the creek."

Getting into motion sounded like a great idea to me. "Okay. I was meaning to go to that market anyway for a little Christmas shopping."

I stood up and we headed down the creaking stairs and out into the weak sunshine of a brisk New Mexico winter.

Ursula looked over at me. "Since opioid

withdrawals last a lot longer than three weeks, I'm guessing that meant you went back on the pain meds."

I stopped near the spot where we had done our qigong a couple of months ago and leaned on the fence along the creek. "In a big way. I knew I couldn't face a year of withdrawals like I did the first time. And, I knew the longer someone is on opioids, the longer it can take to get off of them. I went right back to the doctor's office, and they were more than happy to oblige."

Ursula rested her forearms on the fence and clasped her hands. "So, it was back on the pain meds. How long did that last?"

I pushed off from the fence rail, and we continued down the path. I could see the booths for the Christmas fair just ahead. "This time, it was two miserable years on Suboxone."

"Suboxone is for weaning off opioids, right?" Ursula asked, "But I don't think it's intended to be used for two years."

"I figured that out. And, you're right. It is a good drug to help get off opioids. I'd say a couple of weeks on a drug like Suboxone would be about right. It'd take the edge off the withdrawals long enough to get into a recovery program of some kind, but it's a miserable drug to kick, especially after being on it for two years."

We reached the outskirts of the market, and I could smell cinnamon wafting by. *Hot apple cider*, I thought.

"That's way too long," Ursula agreed. "Especially if the goal is to get off opioids at some point. I guess a patient could stay on it forever and never have to suffer withdrawals."

"For me, staying on Suboxone was a fate worse than death," I said.

We ended up in front of a booth bursting with brightly colored Christmas ornaments made from recycled aluminum cans. Neither of us spoke for a while.

"Man, that cider smells good," I said.

Ursula smiled. "Let's get some."

Survival Tips

The following are a few of the things I did to survive opioid withdrawals. No philosophy here, just practical tips.

Warm Water: Opioid addicts are constantly either freezing or breaking out in sweats during withdrawals. It's a lot like the flu, but it can last for many months. For me, the freezing part was the worst. Getting into warm water helped the most. Hot showers or baths, especially with Epsom salts, are great. Being in a hot tub or natural hot springs is even better.

Towels: There is no way to avoid pouring sweat all night for the first few weeks of opioid withdrawal. I discovered that having a big stack of towels by the bed is the best technique for saving my sheets and mattress from being continually soaked in toxic sweat. I would start the night with a fresh towel under my body. Once that one was drenched, I'd swap towels and repeat as needed.

Motion: Motion of any kind is a must. It's a good way to dispel the skin-crawling. However, one of the last things I wanted to do while in the grip of withdrawal was exercise. Even so, just walking around my home helped. Combining exercise with getting into warm water is ideal. The heat chases away the ice-ants, and the natural buoyancy of the water supports ruined joints.

Distractions: Distractions are also beneficial in keeping the mind from focusing on the misery of withdrawals. My bracelets are a handy distraction technique that I can use almost anywhere. However, getting out in nature to soak up some sunshine would be first on my list. If you can't get outside, there's nothing wrong with a Netflix binge. Just be careful not to isolate yourself.

When you're in the throes of withdrawal, the above practices may seem like pissing on a forest fire. So, my strongest advice is this: do not embark on this journey alone. If I didn't get professional help to deal with some of the underlying trauma behind my addiction, I wouldn't be here today.

CHAPTER
TWELVE
GOOD WOLF/BAD WOLF

Therapy Session

"I was thinking about some of the suicidal thoughts you mentioned," Ursula announced. "Does that mean you never tried—beyond planning to use a storage shed and rental car—to kill yourself?"

I sank into the chair cushion, somewhat taken aback by the directness of the question, but that's what I appreciated about Ursula. She listened to what I had to say. She had a quick mind and made rapid connections.

"Looking back, I guess I was fortunate enough to get to the psych ward before doing the final act. I was so miserable on the Suboxone that I often thought of just ending it all. I later learned the term 'suicidal ideation,' which was closer to the truth, I guess."

"Closer to the truth?" she asked. "How so?"

"It wasn't that I wanted to die," I answered. "I just couldn't stand that level of suffering anymore."

"Tough times," she said. "Were they hard on your relationship with Lori?"

"Very hard." I sighed. "She told me she couldn't go through another bout with me and the withdrawals, but she put up with one more. We survived it and are stronger for it."

"Drugs and other addictions can be so consuming," Ursula commented. "Non-addicts sometimes don't understand the self-centered attitude of an addict. It's not an excuse, just the reality."

"Opioids became my mistress. I did anything to keep the relationship, including lying. It was like having an affair with the drug."

"I like that you said that in the past tense. So, opioids are no longer your mistress?"

I unhunched my shoulders.

"I am once again a faithful husband," I replied. "Lori and I have been together for over forty years. We probably have at least a couple more decades left, and I'm looking forward to them, but it was very touch-and-go for a while."

"How so?"

———

"You're probably experiencing what we like to call secondary gain," said Doctor Savage. "That may be the primary reason you are finding it difficult to stop abusing opioids."

It had never occurred to me that I might be experiencing some "gain" from all of this. "What is secondary gain?"

"Because you're so disabled by your pain and drug dependency, your wife and other caregivers in your life take care of everything for you," he answered.

"You mean like wiping my ass?"

"Perhaps," my new psychiatrist replied. "More like doing the shopping, helping you get dressed, providing income, and so on. Maybe you even liked gaining attention or pity from others."

"I was constipated for five days last week," I said bluntly. "Have you ever gone five days without being able to take a shit? I don't recall thinking I'd *gained* anything."

"I understand," Dr. Savage replied. "Nevertheless, I'm going to recommend that you take a drug called Suboxone. It's a wonderful discovery. Patients don't get any sense of euphoria, but it does stop the withdrawals, and likely will help with your chronic pain."

Sitting on a metal table in an examination room about the same temperature as the freezer section at the local Safeway market, a new set of chills wracked my body. I began to shiver, and the ice-ants started crawling through my chest. But I heard him say, "stop the withdrawals," and I clung to those words like a drowning man clinging to a life jacket. The mere possibility of stopping the writhing and screaming that made up much of my days had suddenly blocked out all common sense and judgment. I'd been out of detox for three weeks, and the symptoms had not backed off at all.

"How long before it will help with the withdrawals?" I demanded.

"Minutes, but you'll need to stay on the Suboxone, and I'm the only one on the island who can prescribe it. I'm only on the island one day every two weeks, so we'll need to plan another appointment to see how you are doing next month."

"Let's do it," I said.

Doctor Savage had been correct about one thing. I went straight to the pharmacy and within minutes of taking the delicious orange pill, all my withdrawal symptoms were gone.

The contrast was like stepping into a warm bath with a mug of hot chocolate after trudging naked through a snowstorm. I also didn't get the euphoric rush that got me into trouble in the first place.

I made one more appointment with Doc Savage. He was very pleased with himself and refilled my prescription. Then, the following month, the strangest thing happened. I called and tried to get my prescription refilled, but couldn't locate the good doctor. Keep in mind, if I ran out of my little orange pills, I would be plunged into withdrawals again. I knew I wouldn't survive that.

I was transferred from doctor to doctor. It seemed that Savage was no longer coming to Maui. No one would tell me where he went or why he left. I tried to track him down on Oahu, but to no avail. The legalized drug dealer had disappeared into the protective ring of the medical/pharmaceutical world, and a cloak of silence had been draped over the ordeal. I finally found doctors who were willing to give me one refill at a time, so I limped along like that for a couple of months.

By now, I was firmly back in the grip of a series of nasty side effects that seemed worse than the other narcotics I had been prescribed over the years, and there wasn't even the benefit of feeling any euphoria. Suicidal thoughts came creeping back, and it soon became clear that I needed to either get off this stuff or kill myself.

After a few months of no answers, my medical provider informed me that they simply didn't have anyone on the island who could provide any more refills of Suboxone. I would have to fly to Honolulu once a week to get refills and to take a urine test to make sure I wasn't taking any street drugs.

I flew to Honolulu to meet with another expert on opioid addiction who had the ability to prescribe Suboxone. He didn't work for my medical provider, but since their guy was AWOL, the new guy was the only one they could dig up.

Although ill-equipped to help me get off the meds, my medical insurance did provide a voucher for a taxi from the airport to downtown Honolulu. Once downtown, I ascended into a nondescript high-rise office building in the non-touristy part of Hawaii's biggest city.

I got off the elevator on the 12th floor and found the doctor's suite. The first thing the young lady working reception did was hand me a plastic jar with a screw-on lid. She was a perfect blend of Caucasian and Polynesian beauty. Although her striking good looks were a pleasant distraction, there's something about being handed a urine sample jar that undermines any new relationship. She was polite and pointed to the restroom in the lobby. I dutifully filled the jar and returned it.

After a couple of months of flying back and forth, I realized the side effects were getting worse. I had begun to create clever scenarios to end my life, so I finally asked the doctor if I could get off those pills. The answer was always, "Maybe later."

I was on Suboxone for two years.

I was still in chronic pain, constipated, and depressed. I decided to stop taking the meds.

At the next session in the Honolulu high-rise, I asked for help one more time to try to get off the drug and was once again rebuffed. So, I implemented my own recovery plan.

I got my weekly prescription of Suboxone and started taking half the dose. It wasn't like the little pills got me high anyway—that was the point of Suboxone. The drug was designed to get people off heroin or methadone, but it was only supposed to be used over a couple of weeks to deaden the dope sickness.

I knew I wouldn't survive another battle of withdrawals on my own, so I continued to hoard the Suboxone and took just enough to keep the demons at bay. I kept up the subterfuge, pee samples and all, until I had enough of the little orange pills to get me through a 90-day taper at a recovery center.

Therapy Session cont.

"So, you had no doctor to help you get off the meds, and took it upon yourself to fix it," Ursula commented. "Very courageous, but once again, it points out your penchant for reckless behavior. Even after stopping police work, your mind was still seeking the risk."

"True," I said, "but in a way, I hope I never lose all of my edge."

"You think taking risks is a part of your personality?" she asked. "Something that will never go away?"

"I'm not sure. I've always liked that story about the good wolf and the bad wolf."

"Which story is that?"

"I think it's Native American in origin. Basically, there's a good wolf and a bad wolf inside of everyone. The wolf that wins is the one you feed. I think that's true, but I also think the bad wolf can help motivate me at times."

"What feeds the bad wolf?" Ursula asked.

"Fear," I said, "but we need the bad wolf in order for there to be a good wolf."

"Do you mean the good wouldn't exist without the bad?"

"Nothing quite that deep," I answered. "Anger can be a great motivator to get up each morning, despite the pain."

"That sounds grim," she mused. Her green eyes lost their focus for a moment, but she quickly recovered. "I think I get it. I lost a child years ago in a car crash in Germany. I certainly felt the bad wolf. It did keep me going at times."

I looked at the flowers on her desk. Today, they were poinsettias, crimson heads turned toward the pale winter sun streaming in through the window. For the first time, I noticed a small, stand-up picture frame on her desk. I was pretty sure it wasn't there before. The photograph showed a younger Ursula holding a baby in one arm and gripping the hand of a blonde teenage girl.

We sat in silence for a moment.

"Let's get back to the Suboxone," she prompted. "What happened after you hoarded all those pills? Did you get into recovery on Maui?"

"I did. And it was paradise compared to Mahalo House."

Survival Tips

These survival tips draw from lessons learned during that 90-day treatment in Hawaii. It discusses how the physical, intellectual, emotional, and spiritual (**PIES**) are all important to recovery.

PIES is a check-in technique that the counselors used in my group sessions. For me, it was a great tool for getting in touch with how I was feeling and where I needed more attention.

Physical: It begins with the physical check-in. While I was titrating off Suboxone, I felt a lot of physical pain as my brain and body struggled to get back online. However, as the drug started to leave my system, and as I participated in daily (even twice daily) exercises such as yoga and qigong, I started to feel less pain. Yet, it was so incremental that I wouldn't have noticed if I wasn't doing my daily PIES check-in with my therapy group.

Intellectual: I also started to feel sharper, intellectually. The brain fog caused by the drugs began to fade. Many of the therapies at rehab focused on using our brains to solve problems and interact with others. Using our brains in different ways helps lift that fog.

Emotional: Emotionally, I got a lot out of the check-in because my feelings were all over the map. One day, I might feel horribly depressed, in pain, or anxious, but the next day, I might feel pretty good. I wouldn't notice that occasional positive emotion unless I took the time to do the check-in.

Spiritual: And finally, touching base with the spiritual side of things can be very centering. Mindfulness techniques such as yoga, qigong, and meditation are helpful. Personally, I'm a big fan of visiting the Golden Rule on a daily basis. Treating someone the way you would like to be treated may seem like an oversimplification, but, when it is mixed with a genuine effort to stop making ignorant assumptions about people, I feel it enters the spiritual realm.

Although PIES is designed to be used during process groups, I encourage you to do a PIES check-in every day. You can jot it down, but I just do a mental checklist. And it's a great check-in with your partner to see how they are doing. It only takes a minute and it's free.

CHAPTER
THIRTEEN
SURFING THE URGE

Therapy Session

"I've been thinking about that residential place you attended," Ursula said. "The one in Hawaii. Wasn't the staff reluctant to hold on to your hoarded supply of orange pills?"

Her office was a little cold today. It was the beginning of a new year, and the January chill emanated from the big, single-pane window. A shiver coursed through my body, whether from the cool air or my memories of the 90-day rehab stint, I couldn't say.

"They didn't seem to care," I replied. "The nurse even asked me if she could borrow a couple of my Suboxone to give to a young woman who'd just been admitted for heroin addiction. She was going through fierce withdrawals."

"They used your pills?" she asked, eyebrows raised. "Wasn't there a doctor around?"

"It was a weekend, and I guess the doctor they used was unavailable," I said, "but there was no way I was going to let that young woman suffer through withdrawals. No one can get through that without help, and, at the time, it seemed like my Suboxone was the only option for her."

"It still sounds unethical. In fact, it probably was illegal."

"I'm sure it was." I shrugged. "Looking back, that place was a little sketchy. Though, I didn't have anything to compare it to. I did manage to get completely off opioids in ninety days. Or, as one of my fellow patients liked to say, I was able to 'surf the urge of rage and cravings'."

"An apt phrase for recovering on the islands," said Ursula. "What was it like there?"

———

Tiffany smashed the glass beer mug on the granite countertop and began slicing her wrist with the jagged shards.

I sat on the couch watching *Stranger Things* with six of my fellow addicts at a Hawaiian co-ed residential treatment facility. We were in the big dayroom, just off the communal kitchen, located inside a large hut that matched the rest of the gated compound. The whole treatment facility looked like a Polynesian village of grass huts, hammocks, lush vegetation, and lots of rats and centipedes.

Once I saw the blood and noticed that there was no staff around, I had to make a decision: Do I save her life, or do I let Tiffany continue to saw through her wrist and bleed out?

She had managed to get ahold of six sleeping pills and caught the buzz that results when you take six times what is prescribed. In this case, the effects were the opposite of a sleeping pill, and she acted more like one of the hyped-up PCP addicts I'd encountered as a street cop in the Bay Area.

I didn't particularly like Tiffany. She was obnoxious and entitled. She also outweighed me by forty pounds and was pouring sweat like only the tropics and an overdose of Ambien can produce.

In the end, I opted to save her.

I launched off the couch and grabbed the jagged beer mug out of her hand. I strode over to the kitchen trash can and threw it away.

Tiffany then picked up a big piece of glass from the floor and started hacking at her wrist again. Using skills I learned as a cop, I grabbed one of her arms and put her into a control hold, but she was strong and slippery with sweat and blood. I managed to get the shard out of her hand, but then she suddenly twisted.

The bolt of pain shot through my left shoulder that almost made me blackout. I'd had surgery on that shoulder a month before, and it hadn't fully healed.

Police and wayward staff rushed in, and after an

admirable but futile fight against the boys in blue, Tiffany was handcuffed and taken to the hospital. It was a good thing they came when they did. The pain in my shoulder had rendered me useless.

Therapy Session cont.

"What took the staff so long to respond?" Ursula asked.

"Incompetence, mostly," I said. "There was only one staff person on duty, and God knows what took him so long. The place later fell completely apart when the owner started hitting on the younger women. It didn't matter to him if they were clients or counselors."

Ursula nodded, and I continued.

"I liked having the female energy around, but that place went sideways fast. The owner hired a new director, a timeshare salesman whose only claim to fame was attending a lot of twelve-step meetings. The new director added more AA meetings and canceled yoga, acupuncture, and so on."

"I read in your file that twelve-step programs aren't your favorite choice for recovery."

"AA and NA have saved a ton of lives," I said, "but we were forced to attend two AA meetings a day, seven days a week, for months. I attended almost two hundred meetings during that stint of recovery."

"You don't think it works for addiction recovery?"

"Not as a forced part of a treatment program," I replied. "It's great as a community support group if it stays anonymous and voluntary. Not part of a court order."

"Good points." Ursula nodded. "It's interesting to me that you once again put yourself in the middle of a dangerous situation by saving that girl." She crossed her arms and narrowed her eyes. "Did you even think about leaving and going for help instead of risking your life? Maybe try 'surfing the urge' to jump into a dangerous situation?"

Anger made me grip both of my knees until my knuckles turned white. "I guess I could've just watched her bleed out."

I took a deep breath and instinctively began to scan the room. We were silent for several moments.

"I'm sorry, Scott," Ursula said finally. "That was too strongly worded. I admire your courage and how you take a stand. I wish more people did the same."

I felt my shoulder muscles unwind. "If I had to do it all over again, I'm not sure what I'd do, but I don't think I could watch someone try to end their life and not act."

"Our strengths are our weaknesses," Ursula remarked. "You have amazing physical and ethical courage, but it makes you do stupid things."

I laughed. Ursula smiled.

Survival Tips

The healing process for addicts is an emotional roller coaster of epic proportions. Anger and even rage seem to be emotions shared at some point by all folks going through withdrawals and recovery. For me, the constant physical and emotional pain would build to the point where I would lash out like a tiger being hit by a whip.

It's no fun being forced to go to rehab or having someone confront you with your addiction. I felt so much shame from becoming an addict and losing my career that I couldn't look in the mirror. Although a little guilt may come and go in anyone's life, shame tends to hang around and fester, and it usually leads to isolation and other poor coping behaviors.

There are times when too much stress or triggering may cause an overwhelming urge for traumatized folks to inject heroin into their veins, chug a handle of vodka, or slice open their wrists with a broken beer mug. Better to learn some ways to short-circuit those cravings; to ride them out and surf the urge.

Radical Acceptance: One of the concepts that helped with my recovery was radical acceptance. It's all about recognizing and letting go of the bitterness and resentment around whatever unfairness life shovels your way. It's about learning to wake up to your challenges and limitations. It's about living in the moment, even if some of those moments are incredibly painful.

There was an instructor named Steve at one of my rehab centers whose job was to teach us about radical acceptance, as well as give us techniques for surfing urges. The sessions were always held outside in the hot sun. As the exuberant therapist poured sweat along with the rest of us, he would make us close our eyes and pay attention to the subtle sensations of a sightless world.

Then, he'd drill us unmercifully on what we noticed—Bird song. A flag flapping in the wind. Distant laughing. The warmth of sunshine. The sound of our heartbeats, and so on. It was all about learning how to be mindful and stay in the present. You can start with the four-count breath to get relaxed, and then travel to your happy place. Then, just experience everything around you through sounds, smells, and sensations. Keep your eyes closed so the more subtle senses can dominate.

I was fortunate in that I had no craving for drugs or alcohol during most of my stints at rehab, but I did have overpowering feelings that led to rage, violent behavior, and crippling panic attacks. I did have pain-driven moments of such intensity that I wanted to end my life. So, it was well worth learning radical acceptance techniques.

The key is to learn how to surf urges and cravings —even if you get tumbled in the giant waves a few times. The big waves won't last. You just need some tools and techniques to get through the worst of it. The urges only last a short time (as short as 20 seconds), so riding them out like a surfer is a great metaphor. You *will* come out of the tube.

CHAPTER
FOURTEEN
SELF-SABOTAGE

Therapy Session

"Ninety days is a long time to be in rehab. Did you develop any friendships?" Ursula asked.

Today she wore a red sweater to ward off the chill that had seeped into the old brick building. It reminded me that Valentine's Day was fast approaching. That made me think of my wife, which led to a mental note to pick up a card on my walk home.

"I'd say the closest thing to a friend that I had was a retired professional baseball pitcher named Josh. You might not recognize his last name if I told you, but he was a legend in his day. He was in his mid-forties. A handsome devil, with blond hair and an island tan. Think Brad Pitt. Every time we took the facility's unmarked white van—which we'd dubbed the Druggie Buggy—to the store or other public places, he was swamped with fans."

"Do you think he was embarrassed to be recognized by his fans?"

"I asked him that. He said he loved it, and I believed him. I knew him well enough after a couple of months to know when he was lying."

"I wonder why he loved it," she mused.

"He said it reminded him of better days," I explained. "He was treated like a king when he played. Even on one of our field trips in the Druggie Buggy to a nice surfing beach, he was recognized. A waitress from the pool bar of a luxury resort approached us on the sand and told him she was a big fan, and that he could order anything he wanted."

"I'm assuming there was staff with you," Ursula said. "How did that play out?"

"He was a smooth operator. We all got a round of fancy non-alcoholic drinks with little umbrellas and fresh fruit included. Josh was closer to my age than a lot of the folks who were in rehab, and we spent many pleasant mornings drinking herbal tea and talking about life. He was into Buddhism and liked to meditate. He was basically an aging hippy-surfer gone to seed."

"I like him already." Ursula smiled. "What was he there for?"

"He took a hardball to the head and never really got over the brain injury. Plus, he was already an addict. His drugs of choice were alcohol and cocaine."

"Did he do okay in recovery?"

"Not even close," I said. "He self-sabotaged exactly twenty-nine days into his contract. I watched him do it twice. It wasn't pretty."

"Contract?"

"He'd signed an agreement with the recovery center that if he stayed clean for thirty days, he could move out of the lockdown facility and into a halfway house," I explained. "I know that's what he wanted, but for some reason, he would get so close and then throw it all out the window."

"Why do you suppose he did that?" Ursula asked.

"Fear," I stated. "Fear, and a dose of shame."

————

The plastic bottle of urine clattered to the restroom floor.

I stood in line with half a dozen fellow addicts for our daily piss test. Josh was first and stood at the urinal holding the empty sample jar he'd just been given by our counselor, Frank. The other sample—the "clean" one—he'd secretly stashed away in his shorts came to rest at his feet.

"What the fuck, Josh?" yelled Frank.

To my surprise, Josh didn't say a word, which was rare for the gregarious athlete. He just zipped up his baggy cargo shorts, bent down, picked up the bottle of "clean" urine off the floor, and handed it to the lab tech standing next to Frank.

"Do you think we don't know what you're doing, Josh?" Frank frowned.

I liked Frank. He was street-savvy, so nothing got by him. Josh didn't say a thing. It was embarrassing to watch. Shame hung in the air like a thick fog, so after I filled up my own plastic jar, I left and went back to the classroom.

I sat by myself and thought back on the conversation I'd had with Josh the night before.

He'd been glassy-eyed and slurring his speech, but it was dark around the bonfire we lit each night inside our compound.

"I saw you drink that vodka, you idiot," I said when I sat down next to my inebriated friend. It was Day 29. All he had to do was make it to Day 30, and he'd be on his way to the halfway house.

Earlier, I'd been a witness to Josh's clever ruse to secure a bottle of vodka at Safeway. It'd been during our weekly trip to the grocery store to get personal items such as non-alcoholic mouthwash, Red Bulls, and Marlboros. Heaven forbid a recovery center should ever take away caffeine and nicotine.

The counselor who drove all of us to the store was required to check our receipts against what we'd purchased. But there's always a way to beat the system.

Josh was not only charming but also wealthy and smart. Smart as only an addict can be when it comes to chasing a high or trying to avoid dope sickness. He simply picked up his favorite magazine, went through the check-out line, paid for it, pocketed the receipt, and stuck the rolled-up tabloid in one of the oversized cargo pockets of his baggy shorts. Then, he snuck to the liquor aisle and grabbed a pint bottle of high-end vodka. He stuffed the flat bottle in his other cargo pocket, went through the check-out again, and threw that receipt away. The counselor never even saw him do it.

"If I left this place, I'd miss you, Brother," he said as the firelight glowed on his unshaven face. "It's all good. I stole one of the urine jars last week and filled it last night with clean urine. I'll sneak the clean sample to the lab techs tomorrow during our process group."

"Great plan, Josh. Except the piss won't be warm. Frank or the tech will pick up on that," I said.

"No problem. I'll just put the jar between my thighs while we're in the first part of the process group. Then, when we give the sample, the clean urine will be warm."

"Brilliant," I said. "Or you could just not drink the day before the urine test. Isn't tomorrow thirty days sober for you?"

"It is." Josh nodded. "But I'm celebrating."

"You know you're an alcoholic, don't you? If they see you're drunk tonight, they'll kick you out. This would be your second offense, and that means no more slack, Josh."

"Fuck those guys. They're too stupid to catch me. And fuck you. I'm not an alcoholic."

I knew there was no point debating with a drunk

person, so I let it go. I said nothing and hoped he would get away with it, but I had my doubts.

Therapy Session cont.

"So did Josh get kicked out?" Ursula asked.

"Not that time. Obviously, Frank busted him for dirty urine. And that broke his written contract with the recovery center, but they gave him another chance."

"It sounds like Josh was clever, as are many addicts, especially when it comes to beating the system," Ursula commented.

"I liked Josh," I said. "Ninety days is a long time to spend with someone. He loved to break the rules. I don't care for authority myself, but I have a practical streak and found enough discipline not to fuck around like that. He always had a supply of contraband, like energy drinks or candy bars. He even had his own remote hidden away that allowed us to watch anything we wanted on Netflix, including the forbidden movies that showed drug use and violence."

"How did Josh do with his second chance?" Ursula asked.

"He made it Day 29 again, then he got some more booze," I replied. "It was grim."

"How so?"

"That night, one of the girls who was there for meth came to me and said she thought Josh was sick."

"What happened?"

"Josh had gotten hold of some sleeping pills. I don't know why they let folks take sleeping pills in recovery, but this place had a poor tracking system when it came to meds. We would line up, and some of the staff would just pile the trays of prescription drugs on the counter and not pay any attention."

"What did you do when the girl came to you?" Ursula asked.

"Well, Josh's room was upstairs in a raised grass hut. I went up there, and he was passed out on the bathroom floor with a puddle of puke running down his shirt and onto the floor. I could see some of the sleeping pills half-digested in the mess, and you could smell the alcohol mixed with his bile."

"Did you wake up any staff?"

"I did," I said, "but not until I woke up Josh. Fortunately, he'd passed out on his side and hadn't choked on his own vomit."

"What did they do with Josh?"

"Finally kicked him out. He took off with his suitcase the next morning, hungover but functioning. He had plenty of money, so he got some more booze and got a hotel room. He drank himself silly, showed up at the compound late that next night, and begged to come back. It was sad. The police came and scooped him up, but then they recognized him as a former major league pitcher and didn't put him in jail. Instead, they took him to the airport, and he flew home to his family in Southern California."

"Do you stay in contact with him?" Ursula asked.

"No one does that," I said. "We addicts try to forget the experience for the most part. It's all so humiliating. I don't stay in contact with anyone from recovery. It's not like it's summer camp for adults. Anyways, now it's all a moot point as far as Josh is concerned."

"Why is that?"

"It was in the news a couple of years later." I sighed. "Josh killed himself with fentanyl."

Survival Tips

Self-sabotage is one of the strangest results of addiction, but it happens time and again. It doesn't make any sense. It could be fear of failure. Or fear of success. In either case, fear is certainly behind it all.

Re-invent Yourself: For me, the best way to battle such destructive impulses is to re-invent myself. I still occasionally get depressed over what I lost. My previous career, income, and most of my physical abilities are gone for good. Managing addiction, depression, and anxiety are here to stay, but there is a certain excitement in re-inventing myself.

In Chapter Nine, you wrote down all of the labels you accumulated over the years that influence who you are today. This time, write down all the titles you'd like to have applied to the future you. Some examples may include: teacher, artist, grandparent, recovering addict, mentor, chef, mountain climber, volunteer, marathon runner, and writer.

Now, start taking some action steps to develop your future self. Attend a meeting, take some classes, or travel and learn about other people and places. I took an online writing course that helped me develop an outline for this book.

My friend, Josh, in rehab, was an expert at self-sabotage. He had gone from a world-class athlete to a brain-damaged addict in no time at all. It was horrifying to watch him make it to day 29 twice only to flush all his progress down the toilet. He could never be a star athlete again, but with his intelligence and personality, he would've been an excellent coach.

I think the stigma inherent in being labeled an addict adds to the likelihood of self-sabotage. Josh never did accept that he was an alcoholic or any kind of addict.

There's a sense of freedom with such acceptance. In a way, once I lost much of what I had, I was able to gradually let go of all those artificial expectations that I'd built around my life. I call it lowering the bar.

Unrealistic expectations are unhealthy for anyone. Although it's always a work in progress, acceptance is your best defense against self-sabotage. The cards have been dealt; the best you can do is play your hand well.

CHAPTER
FIFTEEN
BEING GOOD

Therapy Session

"You were successful in eventually getting off the opioids," Ursula said, "and now, you've been clean for years. You do know how phenomenal that is, don't you?"

Although my therapist's office had become a place of refuge, it was still winter, and an all-too-familiar shiver ran through me.

"I do know that," I replied. "I also know that I would never survive another round with opioids—and that's a huge motivator."

Ursula pulled down the sleeves of her olive-green top. She was wearing a light gray fleece vest that complemented the silver in her fine blond hair. "It's good that you're aware of the fragility of recovery," she said.

"I am. All too aware. Last week, I told you I don't

stay in contact with anyone from my rehab days. One of the reasons is that so many of them either kill themselves or overdose. And many of those supposed overdoses were really suicides. The people just wanted to stop suffering. Some of the folks I knew at rehab reached out to me a couple of times, but whoever I spoke with seemed compelled to give me a list of who either committed suicide or went out."

"Went out?" Ursula leaned forward. "You mean started taking drugs again?"

"Or cutting, or gambling, or not eating, or staying in violent relationships. Or just simply falling off the radar, which could be any number of things."

"Or, so successful in their recovery, that they turned inward for a while to heal?"

"Some people get their act together," I said. "I just wish there were more of us."

"Us?" Ursula repeated, with one of her brightest smiles. "You said 'us.' I'm so glad you see how far you've come. So, changing direction a little. What did you do after the 90-day rehab?"

"Hawaii is really expensive, and my wife had to work full-time if we wanted to stay. It was becoming clear that I still needed a certain level of care, especially when I was hurting so badly that I couldn't even dress myself. Besides, I was starting to associate bad feelings with the islands. So, we decided to return to the mainland and get back into the RV life we'd done in years past. We traveled around the country and volunteered at some National Parks. I was still struggling. Still suffering from chronic pain and depression."

"How long did you travel like that?"

"A couple of years, I guess. It wasn't all bad. We stayed at some beautiful places like Sequoia National Park and some natural hot springs campgrounds in the Colorado Rockies. Still, during that time, I never really got to the underlying trauma behind my suffering. I just stumbled from one crisis to another."

"You also said it wasn't all bad. How was it not bad?"

"Well, the nature was phenomenal," I replied. "I connected with some folks now and then who had it rougher than I did. Some had serious medical problems with zero resources to fix them, but they were trying their best. It was both inspiring and heartbreaking. I learned a lot about empathy and compassion."

One particular story came to mind.

———

A heroin addict stole my homemade minestrone soup. A despicable act in any circumstance, but in this case, I was dropping off the soup for Jimmy, who didn't have any teeth and couldn't chew very well.

I'd met Jimmy a few months earlier at a campground in southwest New Mexico—this campground is blessed with an abundance of natural hot springs. I was in my favorite spring, all by myself, enjoying the azure skies unique to this isolated part of the country. The mineral-laden water seemed to draw tension from my battered body.

"Hate to interrupt your peace, friend," said a voice full of gravel. "Name's Jimmy."

Jimmy was as lean and tough as the gnarled mesquite trees surrounding the hot springs. Even his deeply tanned, weathered skin matched the trees' leathery bark. He wasn't young by any means. A mass of matted dreadlocks draped down his back, and his impressive beard was gun-metal gray. He reminded me of an ancient coyote, wild and strong, but well past his prime.

I lived in a small town, not far from the campground where I'd met Jimmy. It turned out that he also lived in town. He had his little motorhome parked in the side yard of a friend and was trading free rent and electricity for fixing up the friend's house.

Jimmy is one of those guys who can build a home from the ground up and even create the artwork to adorn the walls. He's a "give you the shirt off his back" kind of person. He'd already gifted me a rock with a nicely done lotus flower engraved on it and refused to take any money for it. That's why I found myself delivering minestrone to his home.

I had the container of soup in a big plastic bag along with a note in case Jimmy wasn't there. As I walked up to his motorhome, an unkempt young man was lurking around the back of the little RV. He wore a heavy, dark-blue jacket, despite the pleasant, sunny weather typical of a New Mexico fall. It looked four sizes too big. A gray, knit cap covered his head.

"Good morning," I said with a smile. "I'm just dropping off some food for Jimmy." I didn't want to seem like I was trespassing. I had no idea how many people lived in the big house just a few feet from Jimmy's rig, or even who they were.

I knocked on the motorhome door, and there was no response.

My new acquaintance stared at me for a moment and then smiled. Although he had more teeth than Jimmy, the ones he had were blackened. It was a diabolical smile. He didn't say a word and wandered out of the yard.

I set the food at Jimmy's door and left.

A couple of days went by, and I saw Jimmy downtown at the food co-op. We had a short conversation, but to my surprise, he didn't mention the delicious soup I'd dropped off. If you knew Jimmy, the first thing you'd expect is a big, heartfelt thank you, and maybe another engraved rock.

I just had to ask. "Jimmy, did you get the soup I left at your RV the day before yesterday?"

He gave me a blank look. "What are you talking about, Brother?"

"I made a big batch of minestrone and wanted you to have some to thank you for the rock you gave me."

Recognition dawned in his sky-blue eyes. "I bet that little thief took it."

An image of the young man skulking around

Jimmy's RV popped into my mind. "Does your thief have black teeth?"

Jimmy snorted in disgust. "That he does. He's a heroin junkie, and he's been stealing my carpentry tools to support his habit. I had buddies in Nam who got hooked on smack, and they got off it. This guy could too, but he's a weak sombitch."

Therapy Session cont.

"What did you say to Jimmy?" Ursula asked.

"Nothing. It was one of those all-or-nothing things. I didn't have the energy."

"You felt sympathy for Jimmy, but you felt empathy for the soup thief," she said.

Still a bit chilled, I crossed my arms. "Exactly. Unlike Jimmy, I've never gone hungry a day in my life. But I knew what it was like to be dope sick. I knew the thief and I were the same."

"In what ways?"

"We were both opioid addicts and would do absolutely anything to get the drug and avoid withdrawals," I replied. "I knew that the only difference between me and Black Teeth was that I had more resources and didn't spend all my money on heroin. I could afford to buy food."

"So, you weren't mad at the guy?"

"I make great soup, so that pissed me off. But, no,

I wasn't mad at all. I was a little miffed at Jimmy for being so hard on the guy, but I get it."

"Get what?"

"The guy was stealing Jimmy's tools. He needed them to make a living, and he was barely doing that."

Survival Tips

If I were to pick out one thing that benefited me the most during the later stages of recovery, I'd say it was helping others. As I've mentioned in earlier chapters, you must be well in order to do good. Empathy, compassion, and serving soup at the local homeless shelter are great for the healing process. However, serving is an endeavor best left for when you have the physical and emotional energy to give without risking your own health.

Being Good vs. Doing Good: Being good instead of doing good may be all you can manage during the early stages of the recovery journey.

I'm tall and look somewhat fit. So, I always feel a little guilty when I'm at a gathering or meeting that requires setting out a bunch of chairs for everyone, along with putting those chairs away at the end of the meeting. It's probably my imagination, but it feels like people are glaring at me as I kick back while some frail old guy is struggling to lift 20 chairs. I could swear I've heard the word "jerk" whispered behind my back. I find myself wanting to announce that I have bad knees and a bad back and can't lift anything over 10 pounds.

Even so, there are always little things I can do, like holding a door open or letting someone go in front of me in the grocery line. Or even just offering a smile. The simplest acts of kindness and consideration can make someone's day a little better.

Taking a Stand: Taking a stand is uncomfortable for most people. I get that, but part of my healing process was about the plummet my self-worth and self-esteem had taken. Putting into practice my personal morals and ethics helps me feel better about myself and my interactions with the rest of the community. Standing up for my beliefs, or for the rights of someone who has been marginalized by society, is empowering.

In the above minestrone soup story, I made a decision—based on my energy at that time—to not engage Jimmy in a debate on the stigma and misconception surrounding opioid addiction. Part of that decision was taking into account Jimmy's unique personality and unfortunate circumstances, but mostly, the truth was simply that I wasn't up for it.

Pay it Forward: If someone does you a favor or

helps you out in some way, just be gracious and thankful. You can pay it forward when you are able.

CHAPTER
SIXTEEN
TRANSFORMATION

Therapy Session

A cloud of blue and white hydrangeas stood tall in a cut-crystal vase. A sure sign that spring was on the way. In my corner of New Mexico, that meant plenty of wind.

Ursula was wearing a white shirt, collar turned up, and a dove-gray pencil skirt. The shirt was slightly masculine, but didn't look so on her frame. Big, silver hoop earrings added a casual flair. I saw a black leather jacket hanging on a rack near the door.

"Last week you said that you stumbled from one crisis into another," she said. "Are you feeling up to expanding on that a bit?"

"It was brutal," I replied. "I continued to suffer from horrible back and knee pain, and that led to poor sleep, which led to depression. I tried a lot of interventions, mostly steroid injections all along my spine and in other joints. Then, I came down with a case of shingles."

Ursula grimaced. "Very painful, I understand."

"Very. The shingles were likely activated by the steroids. I was miserable, and thoughts of suicide started creeping back into my mind. I remember lying in bed one night and thinking that if I dressed in dark clothing, I could go lie down on the nearby railroad track and the dark clothes would not only be hard to see, but the blood wouldn't be as obvious for the first responders who had to clean up the mess."

"Dark thoughts," Ursula commented. "It sounds like it all came to a head when you settled down in New Mexico. Can you talk about that?"

I felt my shoulders tense up and raise toward my ears. Tears filled my eyes. They always did when I thought about what I'd almost done to my wife and family.

Ursula leaned forward in her chair. "We don't have to do this. It does not have to be today, but it would be good to shed some light on what was happening in your life at that time."

I sprang to my feet. "I never want to talk about it. I never want to think about it." I took three long strides to the big window and looked out without seeing. "Can we get outside for a few minutes?"

"I think that's a great idea." Ursula stood and grabbed her jacket. "Gough Park is just down the street."

I put on my 49ers sweatshirt, and we were on our way. The spring winds were in full swing, and the ever-present blue skies were the kind of pure, deep blue that can only be found far away from the haze surrounding big cities. My counselor and I remained in a comfortable silence, but I was still wiping a few residual tears from my eyes.

We reached the park and headed across the expansive, tree-studded lawn to a deserted, bright white gazebo where we sat on a wooden bench. I took a deep breath, let it out, and dug right in.

"In a nutshell," I said, "I fell into such black despair that I begged my wife to let me die. She knew more than anyone the intensity of my suffering over the past couple of decades, so she agreed. It was a nightmare for both of us."

"How do you mean?" Ursula asked.

"I convinced her to let me register for a program in Europe where they have legalized death with dignity for extreme cases."

"Assisted suicide?"

"Yes. That's a better description," I replied. "It's not about dignity at that point. It's about ending the misery."

She looked out over the big lawn for a moment and then turned toward me. "Yet you ended up having your wife and counselor get you to the behavioral health unit at the hospital."

"I did."

"What was that like?"

"What brought you here today? And keep it short," said the petite emergency room nurse. She stared at her form, didn't make eye contact, and wrote furiously. We stood in a small, cramped triage room just off the entrance to the ER at my local hospital.

"Well, I have major depressive disorder and severe anxiety. I can't sleep at all, and I'm in constant pain. I talked to my counselor, and she said—"

"I said make it short," snapped the nurse. She wore teddy bear scrubs, a juxtaposition to her demeanor. Not what I'd anticipated when my wife had talked me into going to the hospital.

"I want to kill myself," I stated simply.

She stopped scribbling, looked up at me, and smiled. It changed her whole persona. In an instant, she went from Nurse Ratched to Florence Nightingale.

"You need to let Jesus Christ fill the hole in your life," said the triage nurse as she placed a palm over her heart.

Again, it wasn't what I expected to hear from the staff at a professional medical center. What if I were Buddhist or Jewish, Hindu, or an atheist? I mean, I have no problem having Jesus fill the hole in my life, but maybe it could wait until after I was admitted to the hospital.

"How are you going to end your life?" she asked sweetly.

"By flying to Europe and having my wife hold my hand while they inject me like a death row convict."

Apparently satisfied with my answer, the nurse

checked a box on the form just as a beefy orderly—accompanied by a skinny security guard—arrived, put me in a wheelchair, and carted me off to the rubber room in the ER. The mute orderly wheeled me into the room, and I climbed onto the bed. The orderly left without saying a word.

It wasn't really a room, and it wasn't really rubber. It was more of an alcove where the guard took up a position on a chair ten feet from my bed. Because I was a suicide risk, they left the curtain open.

Another nurse strode up. She was older and had smile lines creasing her face.

"Hi, hon," she said with genuine pity in her eyes.

She reminded me of one of those friendly waitresses you might meet in a small-town greasy spoon. She tossed me the inevitable backless gown that gave me flashbacks of my stays at the psych ward in Hawaii. "Go ahead and put this on. The psychiatrist will be here right away, and we'll get you admitted to the behavioral health unit."

Right on cue, the psychiatrist, who turned out to be a psychiatric nurse practitioner, showed up and, after a brief evaluation, admitted me to the behavioral health unit. She bid me farewell, and the same beefy orderly popped in.

"Sorry, man," he said. "We have to do a strip search before I take you to the BHU."

"I understand," I told him. Since I was already only wearing a backless gown, a strip search wouldn't be too much of a stretch. I climbed out of bed and noticed the security guard had gotten off of his chair to watch the show.

Right when I turned around and spread my butt cheeks, the holy triage nurse barged in and set a small red book on my bed.

"That's the Book of John," she said. "You have to read it." Then, she bustled away.

Moments later, my intimate new friend, the orderly, put me back in the wheelchair and wheeled me to BHU, which was a secure unit in the middle of the main hospital building. This would be my home for the next six days. It was a small unit that boasted a large day room where we ate our meals, watched TV, and did most of our therapy sessions together.

Patients moved in and out of the unit every day, but I got to know a few of them during my stay. One of the patients was a severely disturbed 20-year-old man named Jared. He constantly recited, "Bite Mom, scratch Mom, harass Dad, bite Dad, harass Grandma, bite Dad, scratch Mom, bite Dad, bite Mom…" and so on and so forth. Jared rarely shut up, but when he did, he stared at me with the soulless black eyes of a shark.

Another patient was a lady who was in for slitting her wrists. She showed me a horrible, swollen human bite mark on her forearm and nodded toward the soulless 20-year-old. She went on to tell me Jared had also bitten one of the nurses a couple of days ago.

I decided to keep my eyes on Jared. On my fifth day at the BHU, I was beginning to feel better mentally, but I still didn't have a handle on the physical pain. I was in the dayroom with my fellow patients, sitting in a chair in the far corner, watching *Jurassic Park* on the television. I watched the T-Rex open its great maw of sharp teeth and release its mighty roar.

Ironically, the biter suddenly appeared at the day room entrance. We made eye contact, and then he sprinted at me with his arms spread wide, eyes wild, and mouth wide open. He ran at me so fast that, before I could react, he was on me and pinned me against the large armchair.

Jared lunged his head at me and tried to bite my face, neck, and chest. I dodged as best as I could, my hands gripping his beefy shoulders. I heard his teeth gnash as they grazed my scrubs. Seeing no staff nearby, I used my right foot to push him away. I stood up, spun him around, and pinned him against a pillar with my right hand on the back of his neck and my left hand on his back.

Still no staff.

I turned to my fellow patients and yelled, "Get someone now!" All that did was get them on their feet, running around in circles like a scene out of *One Flew Over the Cuckoo's Nest*. It was complete chaos.

Finally, a group of orderlies burst into the room. I walked Shark Boy over to them, and as he looked over his shoulder at me, I could see in his eyes that the fight wasn't over. He reached up and tore two deep gouges down the back of my left hand with his fingernails. I handed him off to the staff and left the room. I made it to my room and rinsed the blood off my hand, and that's when I heard a scream that was so loud and full of terror, I can hear it to this day. Jared had locked his teeth deep into a nurse's thigh.

I stayed in my room and lay down, but was unable to forestall a panic attack. My heart started to hammer in my chest, and my pulse became wildly erratic and irregular. Since I was no longer young, I was fearful of a heart attack. I went to the nurses' station and told them about the anxiety attack. They took my vitals and saw the irregular heartbeat. They also did an EKG and gave me a med for anxiety.

Needless to say, I checked out of there as fast as I could.

Therapy Session cont.

I looked down at the cement floor of the gazebo and felt fresh, hot tears leak down my cheeks. I took a few slow breaths, looked up, and thought I saw a little moisture in Ursula's eyes. I blinked a few times. Maybe it was just my own tears I saw.

We sat in silence for a moment, which was fine with me. In the past, even thinking about that assault threw me into a full-blown anxiety attack.

"Are those scars on the back of your hand from the biter?" Ursula asked.

"They are," I said. "A little reminder of the attack. The police showed up, but I declined to press charges.

The young man had the mental capacity of a four-year-old. I guess I felt sorry for him."

Ursula stood up and walked a few feet onto the lawn. She slipped off her shoes and stood barefoot in the cool grass, which didn't faze me at all. Anyone who lives in the desert knows how rare it is to find a lawn.

"Still," she said. "That place should've been closed down for incompetence and for being a serious danger to patients and staff."

"That's what happened. I wasn't the only victim. The county finally closed them down."

"Good," Ursula said. "I remember from your medical screening that you had to have surgery on your left knee after leaving that awful place. Did that happen because of the fight with the biter?"

I resisted the urge to take off my Crocs and join her on the lawn. "It did," I replied. "After I kicked him away with my right leg, I was still trapped in that big armchair. My only option was to push up and off with my left leg. It tore the cartilage, but adrenaline got me through it."

"So, you checked out of BHU. What happened then?"

"I was completely stuck in fight or flight mode. It was like a permanent panic attack, and it took three weeks for my heart to calm down. My primary doctor even put me on blood pressure medication because my blood pressure was through the roof. Then, my wife and a friend found the trauma recovery center in Arizona, and things slowly started to turn around."

Survival Tips

A few years ago, I watched a big black dog get launched out of the back of a pick-up truck when the driver had to hit the brakes. I saw it tumble through the air, smack the street, and roll a few yards. The dog stood up, shook like it was shedding water after a swim in the lake, and trotted off to find its owner.

I think we often forget that we are animals, just like that dog, but our large brains get in the way of our natural instincts. Animals are attacked all the time, but we don't see them lining up for therapy. All too often, we shove that anxious energy down and store it until it festers into a disease or a disorder. That dog literally shook off the excess energy that helped it survive the accident.

The assault I survived at the BHU changed my life. It woke me up and snapped me out of my despair. Although I wouldn't recommend something so dangerous, it took an attack of that severity to make me realize that I didn't want to kill myself.

My survival instincts were alive and well.

However, it wasn't the attack that set me on a healing path. It was my response. If I had been badly maimed or even had someone rescue me from that maniac, I may not have regained my drive for life. It was because I fought off my attacker and "won" the battle. I was able to control the biter and take him over to the staff. I was able to discharge some of the energy around the attack and use it to survive.

Since primal screaming is alarming to everyone around us and is hard on the throat, here are some ways to shake off the trauma instead of storing it and ignoring it.

Drumming: I was (am?) an adrenaline junkie. I've always had the need for speed and was drawn to police work and other dangerous situations. But then, a series of injuries to my body and brain limited my ability to discharge stress through sports or other physical outlets. So, I joined a drumming circle. It felt so good to let loose like that. The physicality of the pounding, the rhythm with the other drummers, and the vibrations pulsing throughout the room helped me let go of my thinking brain and dive into the primal beat of the drums. I now have my own drum.

Support Groups: Support groups are a great way to process trauma, tell your story, and wake up to the fact that you're not alone on this journey. Unlike process groups, support groups don't have to be formal or specific to addiction. Churches often have such outreach, and twelve-step programs offer an abundance of support that can be found almost anywhere in the world. Men's groups and women's groups are safe environments, especially for men who are often reluctant to express their emotions.

Process Groups: I mentioned primal screaming above, and that is an actual technique I experienced in a process group during one of my residential rehab stints. Whether as a drug rehab inpatient or as part of your outpatient recovery, process groups are a big part of "processing" trauma. They can be very intense, but when run by a competent mental health therapist, they are invaluable.

Anything that lets you process your trauma, instead of shoving it down to fester, will help you to let go and move on with life. I don't think I will ever completely forget that attack at the BHU, but when I think of it now, it's more of a hazy, unpleasant memory. Due to my processing and healing work, this memory is no longer a trigger for a major PTSD episode or full-blown panic attack.

PART THREE

Journey to Recovery

CHAPTER
SEVENTEEN
LOCKDOWN

Therapy Session

Easter was on its way. It was still windy, but summer wasn't far off, and that was fine by me. My therapist was battling against the spring chill in another sweater. This one was a lightweight lavender affair.

"You said things started turning around when you made it to the Arizona facility," she said. "What did you mean by that?"

"Sometimes I wish I were still back there," I admitted. "It was a great place. Fantastic food, pool, spa, massage room; you name it. I became a bit institutionalized, being so well cared for. Didn't have to cook or worry about anything like turning off the bathroom faucet or even flushing the toilet. It was all automated like an airport or hospital."

"I wish everyone had access to that level of care."

"I do too," I said, "and I think a big part of their

success in Arizona was the structure. They kept us super busy from about 5:00 in the morning till 10:00 at night with classes, therapy, and a ton of events, meals, presentations, and so on."

"What was the living situation like?"

"I was housed in one of the lodges with all men. I was fine with that."

"Those places usually have a lockdown for detoxing before you join the main population," Ursula said. "I assume that was the case for you."

I stretched my legs out in front of me. "Yes. I was held captive there for three days, which was two days too long. I freaked out big time in lockdown. Basically, I had a major meltdown and launched into a massive panic attack."

Ursula's smile reached her eyes.

"What?" I asked with a slight grin of my own.

"Do you realize what just happened here?"

I looked around her office. "No."

"Look at how relaxed you are," she said. "When you first started seeing me, talking about that incident would've caused you a lot more anxiety."

She was absolutely right.

————

I slammed my fist on the counter so hard that the young registered nurse on the other side of the plexiglass window jumped back.

"What the fuck do you mean I don't get to move?" I screamed. "I was told once a spot opened up over at the main campus, I'd get out of lockdown. You people are a fucking joke. I want to see a patient advocate right now."

Someone must have hit a secret button or gotten a code word out because a strapping security guard glided into the lockdown facility and stood by while my rage boiled. I knew if I kept yelling, things would get ugly. I'm a big guy, six-foot-five, and a retired cop to boot. When I fly into survival mode, it's all about the fight, and seldom any flight.

I felt horrible about screaming at the young nurse, but I'd been in lockdown for three days. When I signed up for this place, the staff said it would only be a day or so to make sure I wasn't on drugs or actively trying to kill myself.

My spiral toward the major meltdown started about an hour before:

I'd gotten to see the psychiatrist to finally be cleared from the lockdown building and move over to the much less restrictive lodge on the main campus. The shrink, although a great guy who nailed my diagnosis, had the unenviable job of informing me that, even though I was cleared, there was currently no room at the lodge. He'd promised to get me over there as soon as possible.

It'd been a major trigger for me, and I left his office feeling my rage building with every step. While walking back to my room, I passed the front counter and saw a guy who'd come in the night before. He had his luggage with him and was heading over to the lodges, accompanied by a nurse.

That sent me over the edge. The result was my fist-pounding meltdown at the nurses' station. My heart hammered in my chest. I was about to have a panic attack. I needed to get back to my room and lie down.

When I got there, I noticed my roommate packing up his large rolling suitcase. He was a fellow cop who had been in three shootouts in his short five-year career. He took a bullet to the leg during one of them. PTSD and drug addiction were just the beginning of his problems.

"Where are you going, Jason?" I asked.

"I'm going over to one of the lodges," he answered. "I'm finally cleared from this fucking prison."

Although I was thrilled for my roomie, I felt a fresh breakdown come to the surface, and I let it loose. I punched the bathroom door with all my strength and sent it flying against the far wall. Not much of a feat considering the bathroom door was a sheet of foam rubber like a giant yoga mat. It also had Velcro hinges, so I was able to fix it later.

"What the hell is wrong, man?" asked Jason. I was a lot older and more beat up than he was, so I think he was a bit protective of my well-being.

"I was supposed to go over to the trauma lodge two days ago, but the psychiatrist told me they were full and that I had to wait."

"Shit. I'm sorry, man. I thought we were going to be roommates over there." And off he went. I was glad for Jason. He was a good guy and had been in lockdown longer than I had.

Feeling confined in the small space, I fled to the big day-room. I stopped for a moment and stared out the huge picture windows that looked out over the Sonoran Desert. It was really a nice place, considering why we were all there. I sat down on one of the many comfortable chairs near an old alcoholic who suffered from extreme dementia. His name was Wally, and he was a retired pharmacist. I'd met him on my first day, and we got along fine. Unfortunately, each time I saw Wally, we had to start over with the same stories.

"I used to be a pilot in Vietnam," he told me for what felt like the fiftieth time. "I killed all those people."

I think Wally occasionally recognized me as a fellow patient in a psych lockdown, but then his eyes would glaze over.

"I'm sorry, Wally," was all I could think to say. I was still fuming, and my heart rate was through the roof. A panic attack was imminent.

"You don't look too happy," Wally observed. "When I was a pharmacist, I took a bunch of pills for that. I don't remember what kind of pills, but they were strong. I could take any pills any time I wanted. I liked the opioids the best."

"I'm sure you did," I said, in absolutely no mood to hear his shit again. "I'll be okay, Wally. It's just that they promised me a room at the lodge, and other guys are getting to go ahead of me."

Now that I had actually voiced it, I was a little

embarrassed at my reaction. Intellectually, I knew I was blowing things way out of proportion. This was a great place and worth every cent. I just wish my insurance had contributed a few pennies.

"They let me go over to the lodge last week," Wally said.

"Then why are you back here in lockdown?"

"Well, they let us have lighters over there."

"And?"

"I lit the lampshade in my room on fire. They didn't like that."

"Why did you do that, Wally?"

"They wouldn't let me smoke cigarettes in my room. You know I need my cigarettes, right?"

"I know," I replied.

My heartbeat became so irregular that I knew I only had a minute or so before the panic attack hit. In my mind, I'd let this lodge situation get out of control. I walked over to the front desk and approached the nurse. Thankfully, it was not the same nurse I had scared earlier.

"I'm starting to have a major panic attack. I don't think it's a heart attack," I said, "but I can't really be sure."

She immediately called for the crash cart.

Therapy Session cont.

"How long before you were able to get over to the lodge after that?" Ursula asked.

"I got a bed the very next day. The patient advocate showed up and saw I had a point, but my reaction was totally out of proportion to the problem."

"Catastrophic thinking," she said. "Did you ever find out what caused the delay to get you on the main campus?"

"Again, it was mostly my fault. Per my request, they planned to put me in the co-ed trauma lodge versus the lodge for addicts. They figured that with three years clean from opioids, it would be best to focus on PTSD and other trauma-related issues, but there were no beds available at the trauma lodge, and that's what caused the delay."

"So, there was a bed at the men's lodge?"

"There was," I answered. "It was an all-male lodge primarily for addiction. It didn't really matter because we all had our customized treatment programs and schedules. As much as I ranted the first couple of days in lockdown, the vast majority of staff were pros. I couldn't do any of their jobs. The tragedies they see every day would tear me up inside, but my perceptions were way off base at the time."

"Very astute," Ursula said.

Survival Tips

Our thinking can get way off base during detox and withdrawal. Everything seems like a catastrophe. And it can lead to completely warped perceptions. Catastrophic thinking, or "Stinking Thinking" is what they called it at all the 12-step meetings I attended. For me, this means not only thinking that everything that is happening is a disaster, but it also means obsessive thoughts on dreadful outcomes for future events (fortune-telling). In my case history, there was evidence of me feeling betrayed and abandoned from a young age. When I thought someone was pushing my betrayal button, I would get into such a rage that all I thought about was lashing out and destroying anything in my path.

It was the shame that resulted from lashing out that really cycled me into a rage that only fed right back into the flames, like the story above, where I slammed my fist down in front of the nurse. The shame I feel from behaving in that manner can start me spiraling toward a panic attack.

Once you realize that your thinking may be way off, watch out for the following traps.

Triggers: What sets you off? For me, it is feelings of betrayal and/or abandonment. During the psychiatrist appointment in lockdown, I was triggered when the doctor told me that there was no room at the inn. The irony of the situation was that the man had just done an excellent job of taking a deep look at my convoluted history and coming up with a diagnosis. We had even identified how perceived betrayals and a sense of being abandoned had shaped my childhood values. Then, he gave me the bad news about the lodge, and it was like all the air had been sucked out of my balloon of burgeoning hope. That trigger led to a major panic attack that found me on a gurney next to the crash cart.

Knowing your triggers has a twofold benefit. First, you can try to avoid them. When that's not possible and something sneaks in, you can learn to recognize that you are triggered, and you can take steps to mitigate your response, aware that your perceptions and actions might be unrealistic, inappropriate, or just plain wrong.

Isolation: Isolation is a killer. All kinds of poor thinking can fester. Although it took going to a very competent facility, I discovered the only way to regain trust in myself and in other people was by connecting and building relationships with my fellow human beings. Connecting with other people gives me a truer reflection of who I am.

When I started expanding my connections and serving others, I found out I wasn't such a bad guy after all.

CHAPTER
EIGHTEEN
CONNECTIONS

Therapy Session

A riot of red, purple, and yellow tulips dominated my counselor's desktop. Today was the first time in months that I didn't bring a jacket to my appointment. I was ready for those long summer days that required nothing more than shorts, a t-shirt, and a pair of Birkenstocks.

"Last session, you said that you ended up in the all-male lodge," Ursula recapped. "How did that work out?"

"A lot better than I thought it would," I replied. "I had it in my head that I wanted some female energy in my lodge and not a lot of chest-pounding and farting, but, after a couple of days over at the men's lodge, I began to pull out of my funk."

"What do you think helped pull you out?"

"They had this program at the facility just for

cops, vets, firefighters, and EMTs called Red, White, and Blue. I didn't think it was for me. Also, I never would've joined the group if I hadn't been in the men's lodge."

"Why is that?"

"I was no longer one of the boys in blue. It'd been years since I retired. I guess the bottom line was, I didn't think the active cops in the program would accept me. I worried they'd think that I didn't deserve to be in it."

"You felt that you wouldn't fit in?"

"That's right. I found out later I was stupid for thinking that way, but at the time, I was still devastated by the loss of my career," I said. "Police work was my calling, and I was better than good at it. I flushed it all down the toilet by getting hooked on opioids. For years, I lived in shame about losing my income and letting down my family."

Ursula took a deep breath and let it out. She uncrossed her arms and rested her hands in her lap. "Do you feel that way now?"

"I don't," I said. "There are still bad days, but the shame has faded."

"And you did join the Red, White, and Blue group. How did that come about?"

"After I made it over to the men's lodge, I was still suffering from anxiety, and my rage had only abated to a simmering level of frustration. Then, I was approached by Bang, a cop out of Tennessee. He could tell I was stressed out, and he'd somehow heard through the grapevine that I was a retired police officer."

"Bang?" she asked. "That was his real name?"

"No. We all had nicknames, at least in the men's lodge. If you didn't already have one, you had to keep the name selected by the lodge, which was rarely flattering. He convinced me to join the Red, White, and Blue, and he gave me this necklace." I held up the medal hanging around my neck.

"Is there something written on it?" she asked.

"'Serenity, Courage, and Wisdom.'"

"I didn't think you were big on twelve-step programs."

"AA and NA are good for most folks, most of the time, but not for everyone, at all times," I said. "It's a great motto, and Bang gave the necklace to me from around his own neck. It still means a lot to me. Bang talked me into joining the group, and I ended up having most of my best experiences with those guys, which included everything from an obstacle course to equine therapy."

"And, I'll bet they accepted you for who you are," Ursula guessed.

"They did."

———

"Now if you'll just climb up on top of Detroit's shoulders, Scooter," said Bang. "And Curly, you just climb up on my shoulders. Then Jazz, you, and

Buffalo can grab the tire and raise it up to Scooter and Curly."

My roommate, Bang, liked to take charge—even if it was just a bunch of drug addicts and alcoholics participating in the rehabilitation center's version of a ropes course.

A car tire had been placed over a twelve-foot-tall telephone pole, which stuck out of the ground like a monolith. Our group of mostly middle-aged—and let's face it, overweight—cops, soldiers, and firefighters was tasked with getting that tire off the pole. We had to do it without the tire, or any of us, touching the vertical pole in any way.

"Why do I have to go up there?" I asked. "I'm the oldest and most beat up one here."

"You're also the lightest in our group," Bang said. "Don't be such a wimp." That was true enough. Not the wimp part; that was just Bang's way of showing affection. I was a little thin. My meds had made me lose over ten pounds. I had no appetite, even when tempted by steak, cheesecake, lobster, and an omelet bar in the mornings.

My nickname was Scooter. I've been Scooter my whole life. If you dared to show up without a ready nickname, the politically incorrect guys in our lodge would give you an unflattering one. Just ask Curly—he's covered in hair like an ape, and he didn't provide his own nickname before the lodge got hold of him.

Bang was not to be distracted from his task. He was a young cop in his early thirties. He had a southern drawl and, although not particularly tall, had shoulders like a bull. A hardened, big-city cop, he'd also lost his entire unit in combat while serving in Iraq, including his best friend. The women on our campus loved him, but that's a story for another time.

"Just get up there, you guys. Then, when Buffalo and Jazz hand you up the tire, just lift it over the top of the pole and throw it to the ground."

I looked over at one of the staff members watching us, and he grinned. I think he knew it wouldn't work. But this experiential type of exercise was about working together, bonding, support, connections, synergy, and a little physical comedy thrown in.

This was a real moment of truth for me. I knew I was limited by bad knees and job-related injuries. Climbing up on Detroit's sweaty shoulders in my sandals, where I was expected to stand up without touching the pole, seemed insurmountable. I knew I shouldn't risk a fall based on peer pressure. If I tumbled off Detroit, I'd be crippled. Clearly, it was way more prudent and rational to not climb on his shoulders in the first place, especially when I was sure there was no chance of success with the tire.

Of course, I climbed onto Detroit's shoulders. We collapsed like a house of cards. Fortunately, Detroit was a massive and stable platform, and as the over-engineered fiasco succumbed to gravity and levity, I was able to jump free. I landed on both feet, but immediately felt the stress on my lower back and knees.

I'd been lucky. It only took two days of icing and ibuprofen to bring me back to my normal pain levels, but why did I feel like I had to do it in the first place? I'd done my time in the trenches, and I knew I had nothing to prove. I'd been with these eight guys for a couple of weeks now, and they had heard my stories. They knew I was just like them. Courageous and reckless but committed to helping others, even if it meant risking our lives.

Bang got a scrape on one knee, and Curly tumbled off Bang and hit his lip on the pole on the way down; it was bleeding. Regardless, we were all grinning and laughing like idiots. It felt great. I'd isolated myself from my past so thoroughly that the thawing-out process felt foreign. It was like I belonged and wasn't being judged.

We huddled together to make a new plan. I had to stifle my natural inclination to take charge. Plus, I had no clue how to get the tire off that post.

Curly jumped to his feet and proclaimed, "I got an idea." He ran over to a rope, which was one of the few props our ever-vigilant proctors let us use. He scooped it up and ran over to the tire, which was still on the ground surrounding the thick, twelve-foot pole. Curly tied one end of the long rope to the tire and backed away about twenty yards, holding the other end of the rope in his hand.

"Bang, you and Detroit grab each side of the tire and stand up slowly. Be careful not to touch the pole as you bring it up," said Curly.

I watched from my seat on the shady grass nearby.

It was 109 degrees outside, and my left knee was killing me. It never really healed after that fight for my life at the psych ward in New Mexico.

"Throw it straight up," Curly bellowed.

Like a couple of Russian folk dancers, Bang and Detroit bent their knees in perfect unison. They were strong men, and Curly's enthusiasm was contagious. Then, they both launched up with their legs and tossed the tire straight up the pole. I reclined on the grass, confident of their failure but thoroughly enjoying the comradery.

Then, a miracle occurred. A miracle that would become legend at the facility.

The tire flew straight up without touching the pole. It cleared the post by about ten inches and then seemed to hover as it lost its steam. At that precise moment, Curly yanked on his rope from about twenty yards away, and the tire shot sideways like a flying saucer in a cheap sci-fi movie.

It was a thing of beauty.

We'd done it.

Therapy Session cont.

"Isolation seems to be a theme with you," Ursula commented. "I'm sure you've learned about boundaries in your healing work. Porous boundaries tend to be an issue for women, but with men, it's usually rigid boundaries. You are definitely more of the rigid boundary type."

"I've always been that way, I think. When I lost my health and career, I started to pull away even more."

"From what you've told me, your father didn't let people in either," Ursula recounted.

That made me pause. I rarely saw myself like my dad.

"I guess you're right. I've learned a lot about the rigid boundaries I've erected over the years. I used to think of them like a brick wall. I think all cops tend to keep the horrors of the job at arm's length by putting up those walls. I was distant from others in recovery."

"Letting people in is difficult when you've developed such thick armor over the years," Ursula said. "How did it feel to start building all that comradery?"

"It was exhilarating to have that team feeling again, even if my dad wasn't there to cheer me on," I said with a smile. "It really does all go back to childhood, doesn't it?"

"It does," Ursula agreed. "I think you made a huge leap in your recovery during that exercise."

I nodded. "I think trust and teamwork were the takeaways. It took me years as an administrator to learn to put my trust in others. I was convinced that I could do everything better than anyone else back in those days."

"Do you still feel that way?"

"Not really. I learned my lesson with the tire thing. During the very next session, we faced a classic obstacle course, which we had to negotiate as a team. It included tightrope walking and other crazy things. I made a point of just playing a supporting role."

"What do you mean?"

"I knew I would pay dearly if I slipped off that tightrope," I replied. "Something inside of me had shifted. I didn't need to prove myself by climbing on that rope. It was clear to me that these people respected who I was and what I had done. I'm a natural leader and have even been called 'a cop's cop' by a few people. I finally realized it was okay to not jump in and get myself hurt."

"Glad to hear it," Ursula approved. "Especially with your history. What was your supporting role?"

"This time, I walked next to my partners as they negotiated the rope. It was to make sure they didn't fall. I was taken up by the energy of being a part of something bigger than me, and I was determined not to let the group down."

"Again, a big leap for you," she said. "What was your single biggest takeaway?"

"That it's no longer my mission to be a warrior, at least not in the physical sense," I said. "I can put down the sword and focus on healing myself and others. I can let go and not try to take charge."

"Anything else?"

"Yes," I said. "It's also okay to rely on others."

Survival Tips

Maintaining healthy boundaries with others is important to recovery. Take a look at the following and ask yourself where you fit in.

Rigid Boundaries: I had very rigid boundaries and would rarely let anyone past my armor. Looking back, I think it was a safety issue for me. What if I let someone in and they hurt me? In rehab, I learned how to start shedding that armor. Improved self-worth, camaraderie, acceptance, and trust were the results. Rigid boundaries will only prevent the nourishing connections we all need to survive.

I now know that I can let people past my rusty armor without fearing for my safety. I can be completely honest and vulnerable without worrying about the judgment and prejudices of others. I recommend you try letting people past your barriers. It can deepen connections and lead to a richer life.

Porous Boundaries: While people with rigid boundaries won't let people past their armor, folks with porous boundaries may let people in too much. It can lead to all giving and no taking. By constantly letting everyone in, porous boundaries leave little room for self-care. People with porous boundaries tend to rescue and/or enable others, especially those toxic, energy-sucking types.

If this is you, stop taking care of everyone else and take care of yourself. Set healthy boundaries with people who are trying to take advantage of your giving nature. It will get easier with each try.

CHAPTER
NINETEEN
SUPERHERO

Therapy Session

"I remember something one of my favorite university professors used to say," Ursula said. "We would discuss how being intimately connected to others is so basic to our survival. She would inevitably say, 'Connections are the cure.' I love that."

I nodded my head, stared at the floor with my shoulders hunched, and said nothing.

"What are you feeling right now, Scott?"

I looked up, met her eyes, and relaxed my shoulders. "I never would've started to forgive myself if it wasn't for some of those connections," I said. "During that stint of rehab in Arizona, I began to look at my reflection in the mirror again. I hadn't really done that in years."

"What did you see?"

"A slight gleam in my eyes," I replied. "Like a

spark." I looked back at the floor. "Before that, I was too ashamed to look myself in the eye."

"We are social animals," she said. "Reflection is a perfect word for what you were going through. In a sense, you were seeing your true self reflected in all those connections you made in your process groups."

I blinked a few times and looked out her big office window. "I believe that," I said. "At least, I believe it now."

"Do you remember when we talked about the good and bad wolves inside of us? You said you used your bad wolf at times to get motivated to heal?"

"I do."

"I understand all that," she said, "but when I think about you, I envision a sheepdog. Someone who spent his career protecting sheep against the truly bad wolves. I think about courage. You don't always make the best decisions, but you have heart."

I looked up and smiled. "I like the sheepdog analogy."

"What do you think other people in rehab thought of you?"

———

"You're a superhero, that's what you are, brother," Wrecker said. He was a young and charming man from Los Angeles. He'd been through the horrors of being repeatedly raped by his uncle and was addicted to a variety of drugs in order to cope with it all.

I was in my primary process group at the rehab

center. I had two process groups, which I thought was one too many. My first and favorite was the first responders' group. I felt a deep connection with them, even though I'd been reluctant to join.

However, I also grew to love this second group. I'll admit it took me a while. I was three weeks into the program and had learned to enjoy the two-hours-a-day sessions, even if they were exhausting. We were in our regular meeting room, which was our counselor Heidi's oversized office. Like the entire facility, her office was well-appointed, and she had baskets full of stuffed animals, soft rubber toys, and an assortment of things to hold on to for security.

"I agree with Wrecker," Jane weighed in. She was a sensible, Midwestern woman about 45 years old who, as a teenager, had been picked up by a stranger in her small town and driven out into the country. Her captor had raped her and then dumped her back in town alive, bloody, and pregnant. She aborted the rapist's embryo and was roundly condemned by her family and friends.

"Scooter, you *are* a superhero," she said. "I'm scared to death of most men, but you make me feel safe and protected."

I squirmed in my cushioned chair; I wasn't used to compliments, and it made me uncomfortable. At the same time, it also made me feel like I mattered and that other people cared about me. It was a huge revelation. I'd been so depressed and isolated for years. Now, people were calling me a superhero.

"Shit, man," Wrecker said, as he toyed with the

black bandana he had wrapped around his head. "The way you took down that shark guy who attacked you at the psych ward. You're a genuine hero, that's what you are, brother."

Shannon chimed in. "A police chief with issues like the rest of us, and you sought help." Shannon was a cutter. Her arms were covered with large scars where she'd slashed at her skin. She told us it was because she wanted to feel something, anything. She had plenty of reasons to hate most men, though she didn't hate me. She always had a stuffed animal in her arms, held against her chest like a shield.

I had just finished presenting a dreadful assignment: a timeline of my life. It took me three weeks, on and off, to write the damn thing. It ended up being 26 pages long; I had a lot of trauma to cover. It was such private stuff, but after hearing stories from Shannon, Wrecker, and Jane, I felt like my suffering wasn't so bad.

Our group usually had about eight people in it, but today was Wednesday, and every Wednesday we met with another group of similarly traumatized residents. Heidi's office was crowded with sixteen people.

After I finished my life story and got feedback from the others, Heidi stood up and started writing on the whiteboard mounted on the wall. She wrote the word "COURAGE" and went on to write "COMPASSION, WISDOM, and COMMITMENT."

"Now, I want all of you to get up and go stand

next to the person who most represents these words to you," she said. "I'll start with courage."

Every person in the room huddled around me.

Therapy Session cont.

"I'll bet that made you feel great," Ursula commented.

"That's an understatement," I said. "I was shocked to get all that support."

"They heard your story. Your real, raw story. I understand why some of them felt safe and protected around you. You are a sheepdog, after all."

"I expected some of them to hate cops and hang that on me. Or to hate all men. I was way off base in my thinking."

"Great insight," she said. "Once again, connections are the cure. You discovered that people do like and trust you. Those women were all severely traumatized, but after a couple of weeks, they began to respect you. They saw you for the human being that you are."

"It dawned on me that I'd despised myself for years," I said. "I let my family down. I was a drug addict. I was mentally ill, and I hated myself, but the fact that this diverse group of wounded people liked me—that was a game-changer."

Survival Tips

Throughout recovery, one of the mantras I heard time and again from various counselors was that all addicts suffered from some form of abuse as a child. They claimed that the main reason I became an addict was to cope with an unhappy and abusive childhood.

Not true.

I can bitch all day about my dad not coming to watch me play baseball, but unlike Wrecker, I wasn't repeatedly raped by my uncle and his buddies as a child. Unlike Jane, I wasn't kidnapped by a stranger, raped, impregnated, and then shunned by my family for not having the baby. I still had plenty of trauma in my life, as do all of us who have a little gray in our hair.

Consider the following factors in your life. How many were truly within your control?

Environment: We don't choose our families. And, during childhood, we don't choose where we live or what school we attend. It's beyond our control, so why claim the blame for being the victim of an abusive family or other unhealthy living situation?

Decision/Choices: Here's where a dose of guilt may be appropriate. When it came to drugs and danger, I made some really stupid decisions. That said, I don't need to hang onto the shame. It was never my intent to do stupid things. It's important to take responsibility for your actions, but remember to practice self-forgiveness and move on.

Genetics: My paternal grandfather was an alcoholic, and my maternal grandmother was severely depressed. If you don't already know your family history, I recommend seeing if addiction and mental health issues are in your blood. Again, why play the blame game for something out of your control?

Experiences: Earthquakes, floods, fires, war, and hurricanes are all out of our control. So are incompetent bosses and asshole neighbors. I was involved in a number of violent physical confrontations during my police career that I would've preferred to avoid, and I had plenty of violent experiences before and after my career. Some were within my control, but many were not.

Luck (or lack thereof): Like the disasters mentioned above, I might just be in the wrong place at the wrong time. When our older brother died too young from cancer, my other brother, Mark, tattooed "aces and eights" on his shoulder. That was the deadman's hand dealt to Wild Bill Hickok before he was shot and killed. Sometimes we just have to play the cards we are dealt.

I could speak volumes about brain development during my tender years, but that is in the past. What got in the way for me was the intense shame and guilt I felt over what I'd lost. I resisted forgiving myself because I didn't think I deserved it.

So, what about Wrecker and Jane? Do you blame them for becoming depressed or for using substances to cope with their nightmare? Then why would you blame yourself?

CHAPTER
TWENTY
TRUST, FAITH, AND SPIRIT

Therapy Session

"I've been thinking a lot about letting go of the past," Ursula began. "In your case, you believed early on that no one else was going to protect you. That it was all up to you, and you chose a career that perpetuated that feeling." She wore a sleeveless, olive-colored top that matched her eyes.

I'd learned to judge the weather based on her attire. Summer was finally here, and I'd traded my tennis shoes for Birkenstocks.

"That's pretty accurate," I said.

"What do you think was your biggest obstacle in letting go of those beliefs?"

"Trust," I said. "And maybe faith. Or, I should say, a lack of faith."

"Faith in yourself?"

I looked up at the ceiling and thought about that. "Mostly faith in myself, but I carried around enough resentment to have lost faith in pretty much anyone except my wife."

"How about spiritual faith?"

"The God question," I said. "Yeah, I was mad at God too, but as I started to lift my head out of the fog of addiction, I was able to see God manifesting all around me."

"What do you mean by manifestation?"

"The more I relaxed and let go of trying to control everything around me, the more good things just started flowing my way."

"That sounds like another whole session," Ursula quipped, "but I like what I'm hearing. The more you began to trust others, the more you were able to open up and let them in."

"At first, I was a little embarrassed and even ashamed to share my story. I was afraid to open up to others. Once I learned to trust people, the release was like a huge weight being lifted from my shoulders."

"What do you think helped you build up that trust and faith?"

"So many things. The staff at that Arizona facility kept us busy all the time, which kept my mind off the pain and depression, and ensured that I made plenty of connections. Meditation, qigong, and yoga were all very helpful. Ultimately, it was the comradery of interacting with others, who I learned were just like me."

"How were you doing emotionally?"

"Emotionally?" I asked. "Much better. I was still prone to bouts of depression and anxiety, but the deep despair had faded. Physically, I was still in a lot of pain."

"It sounds like, challenges aside, you learned that people weren't judging you," Ursula translated. "Then, you were able to start trusting those around you."

"In a nutshell, yes."

————

I had absolutely no desire to participate in equine therapy.

Horses are huge. I'm not a big fan of their associated smells, and I guess I was a little afraid of them, too. I even told one of the staff members who was setting up my schedule that I wasn't interested in any horse therapy. More massages would be great, and pool and spa time, but no equine therapy.

They didn't listen. Looking back, I think they did it on purpose.

"All these horses are rescue horses," said a statuesque lady clad in jeans, a white t-shirt, and a cowgirl hat. Her name was Sally, and she was one of the therapists on staff at the rehab facility.

"Can we ride them?" Curly asked.

"No. We never ride these horses," Sally replied. "This one is a wild mustang. She's never been ridden, and she's the boss of our little herd."

I was about to ask, "What good is a horse that you

can't ride?" I decided to keep it to myself because it dawned on me that we were a lot like these horses: no longer able to function like we used to.

There were only five guys from the first responders' group in the arena with Sally the Horse Wrangler. It was boiling outside, but I'd discovered that staying busy was keeping me calm, so I decided to battle the elements. At least the arena had a cover and a mist sprayer in full swing to keep the horses cooled off.

"Today, we're going to meet the horse for the first time and get to know her," Sally explained.

"What's her name?" Curly asked.

"We don't give out their names."

"Why is that?" Bang asked.

"There are clients here who are working on their boundaries," Sally replied. "If we give out horses' names, those clients may get overly attached."

"Kind of like AA or NA," I said, "but for horses. Maybe we should call it N-Neigh."

Sally didn't smile. "Today, we are going to take turns greeting the horse," she directed. "Then, we'll groom her."

At first, I thought Sally was kidding. Was this a way to save money by having the addicts groom the horses? She pointed to a large bin full of brushes, combs, and lotions.

"Who wants to go first?"

When nobody answered, Sally walked up to the horse and demonstrated some grooming techniques. "They really love this stuff, but you have to stay away from their back legs. If you decide to go around behind the horse, either keep a hand on her and stay close, or swing out real wide."

"I'll go first," Detroit volunteered. I was glad he spoke up for two reasons: First, I was working on letting go of taking charge and jumping into things too fast. Second, I pictured the horse kicking back with both huge legs and launching me out of the small arena.

I ended up going last. The mustang hadn't kicked any of my compadres, and some of them could be real assholes. So, I figured I was safe.

"Okay, Scooter. It's your turn," Sally said.

The first thing I noticed when I walked up to greet the horse was its massive head. Our wrangler said that if they push their head toward you, it is usually a sign of affection or playfulness. Sure enough, the huge beast head-butted me and knocked me back a step.

"Just firmly push her head away," Sally counseled.

I stepped back up to the horse and put a hand on her massive shoulder. It was amazing; I felt my entire body begin to relax, like I was stepping into a warm bath at the end of a rough day. She slowly swung her head toward me again. This time, I put my other hand on the side of her long muzzle and pushed. The horse got it right away and turned her head forward. Then, I placed both hands on her shoulders and pressed her slowly back. The sense of calm increased, and it seemed to me that the mustang relaxed along with me.

Picking up on our interaction, Sally spoke. "The

calmer you are, the calmer the horse will be. They are incredibly sensitive to your vibe."

I picked up one of the big brushes in my right hand and began grooming her shoulders, back, and flank. I felt the need to touch the horse again and reached up. Before my hand even made contact, I felt a warm aura of energy radiate through my hand and up my arm. When I made contact, a sense of peace washed over me.

It was weird. I'd been so ready to hate this equine therapy, but I'd never been more wrong. When we were done, she was one shiny and well-groomed horse. She seemed to appreciate the attention.

"Okay," Sally said. "Now that the little mustang has met all of you, it's time to work on trust, and maybe a little teamwork."

She picked up a huge roll of five-inch firehose, walked to the center of the arena, and arranged the flattened hose into a giant keyhole shape on the warm sand.

"Scooter, why don't you go first this time?" Sally handed me a blindfold. "You're going to wrap this over your eyes. But first, grab the mustang's lead rope and walk her over to the entrance to the keyhole I outlined with the hose. She'll be fine, she likes you."

I liked her too. However, I wasn't sure if I trusted the horse that much yet, but I'd already learned to trust the guys in my first responders' group, so why not trust a horse?

I strolled over to the horse and immediately felt

that calming energy. I grabbed the lead rope and held it slack like our therapist had instructed, and the mustang simply fell in line at my right shoulder. I walked her over to the keyhole entrance.

"Now I want three of you guys to volunteer and place yourselves around the big, round part of the keyhole. Stand back a couple of yards. Your job will be to help Scooter—who will be blindfolded—by giving commands to ensure he leads the horse straight into the keyhole and then walks her in a circle around the inside of the big round part. Got it?"

We all nodded our heads.

"There's one more thing: you guys can only use two words. Total. And Scooter, you can't say anything. Just choose any two words, and any of the rest of you can shout them out. Your objective is to help Scooter and the horse make it around that circle, but they can never touch or cross over the fire hose on the ground."

"What two words should we use?" Curly asked.

"Any words you choose as a group that you think will help."

Bang spoke up. "Let's do 'right' and 'stop'."

Sally walked up to me and held out a rolled-up bandana.

"Put on the blindfold and lead her inside the keyhole, walk her around, and come back out without either of you touching or crossing the hose. Think you can?"

Therapy Session cont.

"Did you succeed?" Ursula asked.

"I did. Or, I should say, *we* did," I said. "It seemed that every time I stepped in the wrong direction, it was the horse's gentle nudges that kept me on the path. The guys' instructions were both helpful and confusing, but the guidance from the horse felt right."

"You trusted the horse. That's a big step for you."

"Trust? I guess you're right," I said. "I just kind of let go. The horse was at my right shoulder, and I held the lead loosely in both of my hands. I began to circle to the left, and the horse stopped in her tracks as if to say, 'Not that way, stupid human.' I got it right away after that and started to circle to the right."

"So, she could communicate."

"Exactly. That was the bizarre part. The wrangler told us that horses are social animals and need each other to survive."

"Like people," Ursula said. "And the big takeaway from your reluctance to do equine therapy is what?"

"Not to make assumptions would be one. I was convinced that I wouldn't like the horse thing and that it wouldn't help me."

"Much like you were convinced that the first responders' group was not for you."

"Precisely," I said. "I let my assumptions take over, and they were wrong. I was prejudging the equine stuff before I even gave it a try, but the biggest takeaway would have to be learning to trust and have faith in myself and others."

I smiled as Ursula jotted a note.

"And in horses."

Survival Tips

A good friend of mine, also named Scott, surfs any chance he can get. Scott and I are no longer young men, so I asked him what he gets out of surfing. What motivates him to get up early, drive to the beach, and jump into the ice-cold water? My back and knees ache just thinking about it.

The short answer was that surfing is his way of connecting with something greater than himself.

Just the idea of a shark bite is enough to make me choose other spiritual paths, but I can imagine the peace and calm of sitting out on that board, the exhilaration of riding the perfect wave.

In a sense, the ocean is his place of worship.

My intent here is not to pander to folks' sensitivities or to be politically correct. I simply want to point out that there are many spiritual paths on which to tread. Trusting in something greater than yourself, even if it's simply the collective kindness of those around you, is important to your recovery. If you don't already have your spiritual community, consider trying one of the following options:

Organized Religions: Many organized religions around the world provide a spiritual path, along with fellowship and a sense of community. As long as no harm is done, these established religions are a blessing to many and can provide support for anyone going through the healing process. Try shopping around until you find a good fit.

Traditional 12-step programs: Alcoholics Anonymous (AA) and Narcotics Anonymous (NA) are by far the most popular 12-step programs and can be easily found all over the world. There are also programs for sex addiction, shopping, eating disorders, and gambling. Twelve-step programs can offer a huge spiritual benefit to addicts and other folks engaged in destructive behavior. Besides the comradery, these programs are well organized with clear-cut steps to take on the journey to getting healthy.

Refuge Recovery: It's the Buddhist version of 12-step programs. Since one of my rehabs was in Hawaii, where there is a significant Buddhist population, I was able to attend Refuge Recovery once a week. It was much more informal, and I personally got more out of it than the traditional programs. The meetings included meditations and other mindful techniques that I found helpful in my recovery.

Many people believe that both spirit and God are great mysteries that don't have to be solved or controlled. That's faith. Some folks, like my friend, find spirituality in just communing with nature. Whatever path one chooses, a spiritual bond is the final cornerstone to long-term and successful recovery.

TWENTY-ONE
DO GOOD

Therapy Session

Ursula looked at the faded lettering on my shirt. "That's the logo from the Arizona recovery place, right?" she asked.

I glanced down at my well-worn gray t-shirt. I also wore a pair of cargo shorts and my Birkenstocks; I'd apparently become comfortable in front of my therapist. Summer was in full swing, which meant no socks or long pants for a couple of months.

"Yep," I replied. "When I went to stay there, I wasn't thinking straight as far as what clothing I should bring or how much to pack. So, I went to the store on campus and got this shirt."

Ursula was clad in a far nicer version of my casual summer attire. White linen skirt and a form-fitting black top that I would call a tank top, but it covered a little more skin. Her silver-blond hair was cut short again, probably for the warm months ahead.

"What was life like after you finished the residential program?" she asked.

"It wasn't easy. I'd spent that month in Arizona, which put us in serious debt, but all the experts said I should do about a hundred days in some type of program to build a solid base for my recovery. I followed up my residential treatment with a thirty-day Partial Hospital Plan at the same place in Arizona."

"That's pretty far from your home," she commented. "Where did you live while you were there?"

"The PHP was eight hours a day, five days a week, doing almost exactly what I did in residential. But the difference was that after spending all day in class, I drove my little RV back to a campground to spend the night. That was a huge step because in that situation I could've easily gotten hold of drugs. They didn't even make me take a urine test during the PHP. That bolstered my self-esteem a bit."

"But you didn't get a hold of any drugs," Ursula said, "because you were ready to move forward?"

"It never even entered my mind to go out," I said. "Now, I see what a blessing that was. And, I was really lucky to get into that PHP."

"How so?"

"It was the Red, White, and Blue program that came to my rescue. The psychologist who ran the program got me a full scholarship for the PHP right there at the same Arizona facility. It would've cost me $30,000."

Ursula smiled. "And that never would've happened if you hadn't decided to join them."

"After paying for the residential treatment program, my wife and I were completely tapped out financially, and I was nowhere near ready to make a go at a normal life."

"How do you mean?"

"I'd done a ton of healing, but I knew I needed the PHP to make it all stick, but with no money, I didn't know what to do or where to go."

"That scholarship was indeed a blessing for you and your wife," Ursula agreed. "You said you did your Intensive Outpatient Program back home in New Mexico."

"My IOP was four days a week. I did that for six weeks. The best part was being back home with my wife. It really helped me normalize."

"How did the IOP compare to the Arizona facility?"

"It was a solid program that focused on addiction. Mostly methamphetamine addiction. My fellow attendees were all there by court order for meth, so it wasn't a perfect fit. There were some really hard cases in there. I think they got a kick out of me being a retired cop, but all addicts suffer similarly, and I fit in fine and learned a lot."

"Addiction is the great equalizer," Ursula said. "It doesn't matter how rich or strong you are."

I stared at the old brick wall above my counselor's head and said nothing.

"What are you feeling, Scott?"

I lowered my gaze and rubbed my hands down my face. "What do I do now?" I asked. "I'm doing better, but I'm afraid I'll never be strong enough to do much more than just get by."

Ursula's eyes softened as she leaned back into her chair. "What do you want to do?"

"I want to help," I said, a little more loudly than intended. "I don't want anybody to ever go through what I did, but I tried already, and I failed."

"Are you talking about that peer support program that you signed up for?"

"Yeah," I said quietly. "I also tried taking some university courses on substance abuse disorders. That didn't work out so well."

"Why not?"

"I attended my first class, but once again, I had a panic attack and left."

"Trials and triumphs," Ursula commented. "I get how you think that you failed, but it's those trials we all face in life that propel us toward our triumphs."

"I could use a few more triumphs." I sighed, "But I think you're right about trials. We had one more major trial to endure, and it did lead to some triumphs in the end."

———

Our house burned down to the ground. Not even my iron Dutch oven survived the inferno. Nor did our wedding album or any family photographs we owned. In fact, most of the small southern Oregon town where our home was located was reduced to cinders.

The ordeal began with a phone call from my son, who was living with his wife and two cats in that home. My wife and I had recently settled in southwestern New Mexico after living on the road in our RV, and our eldest was renting our place in Oregon.

"Hi, Dad," Ben said.

"Hey, son. What's up?"

"There's a fire nearby and we need to get out," he blurted.

"Okay, don't panic." In my mind, I was picturing a lone house on fire, maybe a block away. Neither my son nor his wife drives, so I was wondering how they would manage to get away.

Then, I heard an explosion.

"What the hell was that?!"

"I don't know," Ben replied. "Maybe a propane tank or a car that blew up. The whole town is on fire, Dad. I can see the flames about two houses away."

It was then that I noticed the stress in my son's normally laid-back demeanor.

"Okay, don't panic," I repeated. My mind flew into paranoid-parent mode. Ask anyone who has kids, and most would agree that once a parent, always a parent. "What are you going to do?"

Another loud boom erupted over the phone.

"We have our cats and laptops and are headed out the door," he said quickly. That was the end of the phone call.

Ben and his wife managed to wake their neighbor, and the three of them jumped in her car and escaped the conflagration. The neighbor drove them to her ex-husband's home, where they were able to get food and shelter for a few days.

Then, a series of events transpired that not only invoked my everlasting gratitude but also restored my faith in humankind.

I had recently graduated from all my levels of treatment, but still struggled with chronic pain and the associated bouts of depression. Nonetheless, I was getting ready to pack up our little RV and drive from New Mexico to Oregon and pick up Ben and his wife. Then, my other son Sam and his wife stepped in. They drove up from San Francisco to Oregon, rescued our stranded family members, and brought them back down to their home. I was vastly relieved that I didn't have to make that trip. Just driving to the store can sometimes be too much for my back and knees. Traveling across the country with my limitations would've taken a great toll on my mental and physical well-being.

After providing clothing and other necessities, Sam was able to get his brother to Los Angeles while his wife created a GoFundMe account that netted significant cash, mostly from generous strangers, to help out the fire victims. The final goal was to get them to our New Mexico home to lick their wounds while they contemplated the complete loss of everything they owned, but there was still that stretch from LA through the vast desert of the southwest to contend with.

Ben is an artist and writer who has a significant following, and one of his internet friends who lived in Tucson, Arizona, stepped in to help: a man named Jason, who had never met my son in person. Jason drove to LA, picked up Ben, his wife, and the cats, and drove them to Tucson. I was able to easily get to Tucson for the final leg back to our home.

Once the initial trauma wore off, my wife and I began to take stock of our losses, which thankfully did not include our kids. Not only were all of our family photos incinerated, but so were all those Christmas ornaments both of our families had acquired over several generations.

I was hit hard by the loss of a painting of a wolf done by my deceased brother, Craig. It was the only painting of his that I had. My wife lost all of her jewelry and other family memorabilia that dated back well over a century. I was hit harder when I realized I had lost a shadow box that displayed all the shoulder patches I'd worn during my law enforcement career, my chief of police badge, and a Medal of Valor that I'd won for saving several lives.

The flood of love, help, and support that followed the fire, however, was overwhelming. Three long-time friends reconstructed our wedding album using photographs they had taken. My brother, Mark, sent us a few of his Christmas ornaments that had adorned our family tree as far back as I could remember. One of my wife's childhood friends dug up several old photos and sent them our way. My sister-in-law sent us one of Craig's paintings, and my wife's brother sent a box of family memorabilia.

I could not foresee replacing the shadow box that held the history of my service, but God, how I love my incredible wife.

She contacted every agency I worked for and obtained all those shoulder patches. She even found the company that made my Medal of Valor and had it recast. The final act of love and compassion came when my wife got a hold of the current chief of police at my former department.

He gave me his badge.

Therapy Session cont.

Ursula was misty-eyed. I liked that about her. She was able to show some emotion but still remain professional. "That's a moving story," she said. "I envision you and your wife rising from the ashes of that fire, all the more tempered. Two phoenixes."

"In the end, we were able to realize that the things we lost were simply that. *Things*," I said. "Even if they had a ton of emotional value."

"And you shared the ordeal with your families and friends," Ursula added. "If you didn't reach out for help, it may not have turned out the same way. Sharing the burden lightens the load."

"True," I said. "We had a hard time asking for any help throughout my struggle with opioids. Looking back, I wish we had opened up more."

"That's great insight, Scott. And it gets us back to what you can do to connect and help others. Maybe working directly with other addicts isn't in the cards for you right now, but maybe in a couple of years. Maybe never. What about writing? You wrote down that 26-page life story, and it had a big impact when you presented it to your process group."

"I do like to write." I nodded. "During the ninety-day Hawaii rehab, we were required to journal every day. They even checked."

"Journaling is a fantastic way to process. Especially while going through treatment."

"I didn't like it at first," I admitted. "Though it helped me process things. I also found that when I was having a rough day, I could go back and check my journal and read about some days that weren't so bad."

"Good stuff," Ursula commented. "Personally, I think you're wise to not jump into working directly with addicts who are going through all that trauma. At least for now. You need to take care of yourself first. As far as helping others, what are some other things that interest you?"

"I signed up to be on an advisory board for the local rehab center," I replied. "They needed someone who had life experience with addiction and mental illness."

"That sounds perfect for you," Ursula said. "Especially with your law enforcement background. You'll make a great liaison."

"And, I'm talking to state legislators about some of our local needs."

"You're doing well, my friend. Did you know that we've been working together for almost a year? This might be a good time to put more space between our visits."

I nodded. "I guess the road to recovery never really ends," I said.

"It doesn't," Ursula agreed. "But, do you realize how far you've come on that road? Here you are now on your way to helping others on their journey. I think your story is one of hope. I think your story is about having the courage and honesty to ask for help and to move forward."

I didn't say anything. She was right.

And that felt great.

Survival Tips

When I learned that I wasn't ready to work directly with other addicts, it really set me back. I so desperately wanted to help others navigate the road to recovery, but it seemed to be an unreachable goal. It made me re-examine what "doing good" meant to me, and what role helping others would play in my future.

The individual acts of kindness that came our way after the fire were shining examples of doing good. To this day, my heart feels a pleasant ache when I think about the compassion shown to us by those folks. They might not have thought that they did much, but each small act of kindness made an impact, and the combined synergy of goodwill kept growing with each of those acts.

So, how did I find my path to helping others? I discovered that by writing down my thoughts and feelings, all kinds of creative ideas began to flow, and I can serve on my own terms. If I'm battling pain, anxiety, or depression, I don't have to do anything. If I'm feeling good at four in the morning, then I write.

This final set of survival tips is about journaling or any other type of cathartic writing. It was journaling that led me to write this book.

Daily Journaling: Not only an excellent way to process your thoughts, but daily journaling can also be fertile ground to spark creativity and come up with some great ideas. I'm able to dump a stream of consciousness without worrying about the end product. Just that act of processing makes me feel more grounded.

Gratitude Journaling: Gratitude journaling is perhaps the most beneficial type of journaling—you can write down three or four things for which you're grateful each day. It could be anything from a loving spouse to a perfect pizza. If I stop and think about it, my gratitude could fill volumes, and so can yours.

Dream Journaling: Journals are also a great place to write down ideas that pop into your mind and can even be used for processing your dreams first thing in the morning. My dreams dissipate fast, so if that is the case for you, jot them down upon awakening.

Manifestation/Intention Journaling: What do you want most in your life? What is your objective/hope/aim for the current day? Set those intentions by writing down your goals. It's a bit magical, but I've found that if I consistently focus on my intentions, things begin to go my way.

Personally, I would suggest skipping the laptop when journaling. The physical act of writing with a pen or pencil makes me feel more connected to my emotions. If I'm writing near bedtime, I don't have the blue light from a screen disrupting my ability to sleep.

When I'm having a bad day, I can go back and read my journal and remember that there were good times in the past. Which means there will be better times in the future.

CONCLUSION

According to the 2024 Substance Abuse and Mental Health Services Administration (SAMHSA) annual report, one American dies approximately every six minutes from an opioid-related circumstance.

Clearly, we have a crisis on our hands. I purposely don't watch much media because of all the violence, misinformation, partial information, and flat-out disinformation. It's just too stressful.

Sometimes, I become resentful and blame my opioid addiction on bad luck and circumstances outside of my control. It's an emotional reaction to all the physical and mental pain I've endured over the decades, combined with frustration over all the things I've lost in my life. I also recognize that I made mistakes and bad choices that fueled my addiction. As I mentioned in the introduction to this book, no one grows up wanting to be a mentally ill drug addict. The only way I was able to manage my recovery was by working through the inevitable trauma that affects everyone at some point in their lives.

I can't explain why some people become addicts while others may absorb the same traumas and turn out fine. Some folks even become stronger after surviving horrible abuses. Genetics, environment, and experiences all play a role.

Whatever the reason, I did become an opioid addict. All my anger and resentment over past transgressions, real or imagined, won't fix that. In fact, letting go of the past is necessary to heal and move on.

Over the years, I refined my personal values and goals regarding the best ways to manage addiction and mental health. I then developed a set of concrete actions to support those values.

Values and Goals

Wake Up: The first step of my recovery was waking up and accepting the reality of my limitations and challenges. I've seen too many people in treatment who never accepted that they were alcoholics or drug addicts, and it inevitably ended in disaster.

Let Go: Once I accept my situation, the next step is to let go of all the anger and regret over my past. I can finally release the tension and stored stress and move on with the healing process. Letting go of what no longer serves creates the space to feel better.

Be Well: I must take care of myself. Constantly running on a nearly empty tank of energy is exhausting. Improving my physical and mental health helps to increase my ability to handle stress.

Do Good: The final goal is to do good. The Golden Rule is golden for a reason. I am amazed at how much better it makes me feel to serve other people. By helping my fellow humans and other critters, I continue to heal myself. Service is a win-win for everyone involved.

Concrete Actions

Motion/Exercise: As far as taking concrete actions in my life, getting into motion is a great place to start; walking, swimming, yoga, and anything else that gets me moving. Even a few rounds of ping pong or shooting some pool will suffice.

Nature: If my movement can be done in nature, all the better. No one is unaffected by the glories of the natural world. Nature is a great teacher of relaxation and living in the moment. I can't rush a sunset. I can simply watch and behold.

Connections: Perhaps the most important action to take is increasing connections with other people. A sense of belonging and community is essential for us to thrive. Letting people get past the armor I'd erected over the years was likely the most crucial part of my recovery. No one can manage opioid demons on their own.

Service: Although serving others is best left until you get well, it is critical in managing recovery. Serving others not only helps the community but also helps individuals reclaim their sense of dignity and build self-esteem.

Final Thoughts

One of the reasons I wrote this book is to encourage all those family members and friends who have suffered right beside the addict, every step of the way. I shudder whenever I think of the low points that my wife saw me go through, and went through with me. In some ways, I think it must be harder to live with an addict than it is to be one. Our caregivers never know when they may come home and find their loved one lying dead.

Sometimes, for their own health, family members need to walk away, and that is understandable. Everyone needs to take care of themselves in order to be able to care for others.

In my case, my wife and I have an even stronger and deeper relationship than we had before I was having an affair with opioids. I'm blessed that she chose to stay with me through it all, and I feel that I am a better partner because of all the trials and tribulations.

My intent with this book is to also destigmatize the elephant in the room. We need to talk about mental health, trauma, and addiction. Like many of the world's woes, ignorance is the breeding ground for fear and misunderstanding.

I don't get what's so scary about admitting to mental illness. We have no qualms discussing all our physical aches and pains in great detail. Depression and anxiety affect our brains. Brains are physical organs, just like the heart and lungs. Science has proven that disorders such as depression are due to a dysfunction of one or more of our numerous neurotransmitters. Until more of us open up about our disease and ensuing struggles, the stigma will remain.

Behind the Badge can also provide anyone working in the field of addiction and trauma recovery with some additional insight into the minds and behaviors of their clients as well. I never would've made it through recovery without the help and compassion that I received from those amazing people. Help they gladly gave to me, even when I was acting like an ass. Though they don't expect to hear it from their clients, I will be forever grateful.

More and more health professionals are realizing that underlying trauma must be addressed before healing can occur. They are also becoming aware that mental health and physical health cannot be separated, and that is encouraging progress.

It takes courage and perseverance to climb out of the depths of addiction, but it is a journey possible for anyone willing to crawl out of the hole and move upward and onward.

Unfortunately, the disease of addiction rarely goes completely away. Much like diabetes or any chronic condition, addiction must be managed. I hope this book can provide some tools and insights about not only how to manage addiction, but also shine some light on what can be expected while going through treatment.

It is clear to me that substance use disorders tend to go hand in hand with mental health issues such as severe depression, anxiety, and PTSD. I've been told by many mental health workers that my depression was always there, lurking beneath the surface—and the opioids brought it out. Others have said it was the drugs that destroyed my natural neurotransmitters, and depression was the result. The chicken or the egg? It's useless to ponder.

I'm an opioid addict. If someone with my resources and opportunities can become an addict, then anyone can.

More importantly, if I can stay on the path of recovery, then so can you.

ACKNOWLEDGMENTS

One of the biggest realizations I had on my road to recovery was that we humans are not solitary animals. We need connections with other people to survive. The same goes for writing this book. I never could've pulled it off without the help and support of my family and friends.

I'd like to thank my beta readers, Scott, Laura, Pete, and Jill, for their input and encouragement. Many thanks to C.J. Redwine for helping Dr. Ursula Schmidt come to life. And thanks to Nick Halloway for a great edit.

I'd also like to thank my former agent, Lori Colvin, at Birch Literary, and the folks at Harbor Lane Books for taking a chance on *Behind the Badge*.

Most importantly, I want to acknowledge you, the reader. Wherever you are on the journey, whether in recovery or not, hang in there. Things do get better.

ABOUT THE AUTHOR

Scott Fleuter is a retired chief of police. He holds a master's degree in criminal justice and taught part-time at the university level throughout his career. He has served as a consultant to accredited law enforcement agencies across the nation.

He is also an opioid addict and has been diagnosed with Major Depressive Disorder and severe anxiety. His road to recovery included several trips to hospital behavioral health units, detox centers, and long-term residential rehabilitation facilities.

Scott lives with his wife, Lori, and their dog, Ranger. They spend as much time as they can traveling, camping, and enjoying nature.

ABOUT THE PUBLISHER

Harbor Lane Books, LLC is a US-based independent digital publisher of commercial fiction, non-fiction, and poetry.

Connect with Harbor Lane Books on their website (www.harborlanebooks.com) and social media @harborlanebooks.

facebook.com/harborlanebooks

x.com/harborlanebooks

instagram.com/harborlanebooks

bsky.app/profile/harborlanebooks.bsky.social

tiktok.com/@harborlanebooks

threads.com/harborlanebooks

youtube.com/harborlanebooks

pinterest.com/harborlanebooks